THE ROYAL COMMISSION ON CRIMINAL JUSTICE

Human Factors in the Quality Control of CID
Investigations

by **Barrie Irving**
and **Colin Dunnighan**

A Brief Review of Relevant Police Training

by **Barrie Irving**
and **Ian McKenzie**

POLICE FOUNDATION

LONDON: HMSO

CONTENTS

HUMAN FACTORS IN THE QUALITY CONTROL OF CID INVESTIGATIONS

LIST OF TABLES

LIST OF FIGURES

ACKNOWLEDGEMENTS

Important social research often relies on the subject's taking a risk. Acknowledging that risk and saying thank you can usually be personalised. This is not the case here. Nevertheless, we do want to express our appreciation to the senior officers and Chief Constable of the host force for providing access. We hope their trust has been justified. Especially we want to praise the openness and integrity of our informants and thank them for the trouble they took both to make themselves available and provide us with such rich accounts. We realise that some of the talking amounted to more than just providing us with data; it was sometimes a means of dealing with irritation and frustration. We hope it worked. Above all, we hope the effort turns out to have been worthwhile.

We are grateful to the Commission's research secretariat for their helpful advice and for Mollie Weatheritt's comments and editorial help with the draft report. Our special thanks to Mary Spicer and Sarah Tambini for patient help in preparing the manuscript.

We were advised to cut down the theoretical introduction to this report: the decision not to was ours alone but we did refrain from adding a section on cognitive style!

ANONYMITY

In research on accidents and human error at the workplace, anonymity for informants is an absolute requirement. This report would have undoubtedly read better had it been fitted out with detailed case histories. We have resisted this to keep our promises to those who helped us with this research.

At one point we thought we could both maintain anonymity and make the data more accessible by constructing fictional case histories. But we immediately realised that there was no way of knowing whether such fictions would come so close to fact as to be damaging to individuals. We have therefore kept to our original plan of discussing Human Factors issues in the abstract without using a case history approach.

THE RESEARCH

Background

In the study of Criminal Investigation Department (CID) interrogation practice conducted for the Royal Commission on criminal procedure in 1979, (Irving 1980) the field work also covered all other aspects of the investigative process: it was noted but not reported that investigators, usually Detective Constables (DC) and Detective Sergeants (DS) operated with a high degree of autonomy and in most instances were responsible for controlling the quality of their own output.

In this they were helped with advice from superior officers and prosecuting lawyers but no coherent system of quality control existed.

It was also observed that given the remorseless flow of work and the difficulty of the tasks involved, maintaining quality was often a problem and things quite frequently went wrong. Sometimes these lapses were corrected, sometimes not. When errors were not corrected it was not clear whether this affected the outcome of cases. However, it was clear that detectives at that time received little or no training in how to detect and avoid the kind of errors they were likely to make.

While such quality control failures as we shall call them, were often the subject of anecdote, no-one appeared to keep any systematic record of them. It did not appear therefore that there would be any means by which the CID work system could protect itself from the problems it faced by systematic analysis of past problems. Furthermore it was difficult to see how training either of detectives or supervisors could be kept up to the mark if no coherent body of information about the quality of investigative output was available for continuing review and analysis.

When the terms of reference of the current Royal Commission were published it appeared to us that it was high time that a study of quality control in the investigative process was mounted, however rudimentary. It seemed plausible to argue that at least some of the miscarriages of justice which had prompted the setting up of this commission had embedded in them issues of quality control in the CID system. Moreover it appeared likely, on the basis of previous research experience, that the police service might err in the direction of blaming individuals for system failures just because no ergonomic system analyses were available.

A "human factors" approach to CID work is particularly apposite. The CID system is entirely devoted to the processing of complex information and the use of such information to construct formal proofs up to a

1

standard determined by the peculiarly complex and arcane rules of evidence. The value of the product (case files) is determined by the way in which they perform in the hands of another agency (the Crown Prosecution Service (CPS)) in an adversarial contest against a third party (the defence). It is self evident that quality control in such an open system is highly problematic. To what standards are the police expected to work? What constitutes a failure to achieve acceptable quality of output? What degrees of human error are acceptable? It was not until we started to ask these questions and propose a relevant study that we realised that this way of looking at CID work was in itself novel. It seemed paradoxical that with so many ideas from business now being imported into the police service (value for money, performance indicators etc.), the notion of investigative work as a vulnerable and fallible information processing system liable to human error and system failure should seem so alien.

The most uncomfortable part of the concept, when it was initially retailed to police managers, was the idea that police officers making up the CID work system were inevitably error prone under some circumstances; and that a study should be mounted to investigate what kind of quality control problems the CID work system therefore faced.

It was at this point that we realised that the task of proving cases against suspects beyond reasonable doubt clashed fatally with the notion of the human operator as an error prone, fallible unit in an even more fallible error prone system composed of similar units. Far from accepting this truth, the basis of all progress in work design and quality control in other work systems, the police tradition appeared actively to reject it – police officers should not make mistakes.

If police officers cannot be seen to make mistakes like other human operators, then of course their errors, when they are proved, must be malicious or the result of culpable inefficiency. This harsh "personal responsibility" view is one which may account for some kinds of error some of the time but, on the basis of a huge literature on quality control in work systems of enormous diversity, cannot be seen as anything but partially valid. (See for example Bailey (1982), De Greene (1970), Wickens (1984).)

This present study was proposed and has developed as an attempt to demonstrate that the investigative system is prone to certain kinds of quality control problems; that these problems can be described, classified and in some cases explained. That this endeavour can be the basis for designing quality control procedures and training officers to supervise both themselves and others more effectively. Furthermore improved knowledge about the ergonomic character of the CID system can help enhance inter-agency collaboration and point out procedural pathologies.

These constructive aims have to be set against the very understandable reluctance of CID managers and operational detectives to start thinking in terms of their own proneness to system error and quality control failure. The tradition of individual responsibility and blame makes this kind of study tendentious in the police service and to overcome that reaction a number of steps have been taken to protect all those who have taken part. These steps will be described in the section on methodology.

Aims and objectives

The aim of the study has been to build a modest database of case histories supplied by investigating officers where, in their eyes, there has been some kind of quality control failure in the investigative system or in a relationship between that system and the rest of the criminal justice process up to and including trial.

The objective in building such a database has been to describe the kind of system errors which account for the perceived quality control failures and to classify them.

It is a further aim of the study to make a start at accounting for such system errors by examining a range of background variables and the subjective impressions of the investigating officers who were involved in the cases and were therefore well-placed to throw light on "what really happened".

Because a great deal is known about the sorts of errors human operators make and why they make them, even sketchy information in this field can help to focus attention on most likely causes and remedies. In that sense this study seeks to apply existing knowledge to the CID context rather than add to basic knowledge in this field. Via a process of empirical dead reckoning, we aim to identify the sorts of concern upon which trainers, supervisors and policy makers should be concentrating.

A review of training

These aims and objectives necessarily implicate CID and other areas of police training. As we start to move towards a clearer idea of the problems associated with maintaining quality in investigative output, so it becomes natural to question whether existing training provision arms the detective and the CID supervisor with the necessary means of maintaining quality and avoiding system error and failure. We have therefore reviewed existing training materials with these questions in mind.

The review was conducted in parallel with the collection of CID case histories. It was not therefore possible to use the analysis of the case histories to direct questions at the training material. The training review concentrated on the written materials used by instructors and on interviews with instructors. It was not possible to carry out sample surveys of students or observe classes in progress. It is therefore possible that there are instructors who go beyond their written materials and teach more than this review implies.

The scope of the research

The research team had approximately 16 weeks before the report had to be delivered. In the time available it was estimated that about 60 case histories could be obtained and analysed. The investigators providing case histories were also to be interviewed within this timetable.

While a cursory review of the relevant ergonomic literature was possible in the time available, it was not feasible to focus this review without knowing what the case histories would indicate to be most salient. We see this essentially exploratory study as pointing the way for further more detailed work in this field.

For reasons of time, resources and practicability, the study occupies a grey area between research and consultancy. The principle author is bringing to bear on the data experience from consulting work in a variety of work systems and the study is informed by a number of theoretical perspectives. No attempt will be made in this report to argue fully in support of each point made. In strict academic terms this must be viewed as a pilot project in which a way of looking at a given set of problems and issues is introduced. Where the conclusions prove controversial or clash with other views, they should be seen as hypotheses requiring further investigation. Our rather limited aim given the time and resource constraints, is to improve on anecdote and speculation and provide some systematic data where none existed before.

The study is confined to one force. At the level of abstraction at which we are dealing with the data, we do not believe that a similar survey of other forces would throw up different classes of quality control issue, system error etc. However, it may well be true that some forces, because they have suffered from a particular hard case in the past have instituted certain kinds of quality control checks which are not present in the force which hosted this study. Likewise it is possible that our host force makes certain checks which are not considered necessary in forces with different CID histories.

Methods

The way in which we have chosen to obtain case histories owes a great deal to previous research in human factors particularly in the merchant marine

(Marine Directorate HMSO 1991), and the principal author's previous professional contacts with those engaged in research on pilot error.

Human factors research in these areas, lavishly funded because of the enormous costs involved when accidents occur, has established certain principles by which we have been guided:

- only the hands-on operative and his/her immediate work group see what really happens.

- accounts of "what happened" are specially constructed for supervisors and professional researchers/investigators and these groups collude with such constructions

- operatives are the best source of data about how the system in which they work functions especially if their accounts are backed by objective diagnostic monitoring systems. In the absence of such systems however the operative is the only reliable source of data

- where systems of discipline or the threat of economic sanction exist against operatives, accurate data about system malfunction, human factors phenomena etc. can only be obtained by offering informants generous protection and by keeping the de-briefing procedures as far as possible inside the work group (rather than involving managers/consultants)

These principles have been used to great effect in establishing the anonymous help line by which civil pilots bring to each other's attention human factors' crises in flight. They also guided a very successful and sustained investigation of accidents at sea conducted by Bryant et al at the Tavistock Institute. (HMSO 1991)

In this context we took the following simple steps. We recruited an experienced ex regional crime squad detective recently invalided out of the service who had a research interest and an excellent academic record.

Having discussed the aims of the study, he quite naturally and rightly asked to be allowed to operate entirely alone without interference from outsiders.

In a preliminary feasibility study, he confirmed that the focus of information was DC's and DS's and he therefore set up a planned series of individual meetings at which detectives were invited to bring forward and discuss case histories which they thought met our criteria for inclusion in the study.

Each case history indicated a case file which was reviewed after an initial interview. If necessary the person who provided the case history was seen again. If appropriate others involved were also interviewed if they were willing.

In each interview the researcher explained first how anonymity would be maintained, and how case histories would be analysed so that the report would not contain readily identifiable stories.

In particular participants had explained to them the theoretical position taken by the research eg. that the interest was in system character-istics, quality control and human factors not in looking for ways of allocating blame for what had happened in the cases that would be brought to our attention.

The quota sample of 60 cases was determined by the research timetable. This sample was nonetheless considered adequate for analytic purposes. The case sample size used by the principal author in his study of interrogation for the Royal Commission on Criminal Procedure provided a bench mark in this regard (*op cit*).

The sampling procedure was as follows:

the relevant population was defined as all divisional CID officers in the force with day to day responsibility for routine case handling (in effect all DC's and DS's). The researcher made preliminary contact with each member of the population, explained the study and allowed each detective to self select into the sample on the basis of having or not having an appropriate experience (case) to offer. The collection of cases followed an approximation to a random walk around the force CID.

Biases in sampling

In theoretical terms this method of data collection creates an undetectable level of avoidance: that is detectives with important data to offer could simply avoid being involved without the research team finding out. However, the files/cases on which this study is based are available to other agencies. To check that the CID were not selecting their own particular brand of issues to bring to notice, we also asked the Crown Prosecution Service to offer their own list of cases and checked the contents of these against those notified by the CID. We also checked with more senior ranks to see that notorious cases were not being left out of the sample because no-one wished to own them.

Once confidence and trust were established, the range of material produced belied any attempt at censorship. Our final judgement is that the participants in the study have been extraordinarily honest and open. But as always validation will depend on more studies using alternative methods.

Analysis

From each case history we have extracted details of the offence, details of the evidence produced to prove the case and on which the decision to charge was based. We have, wherever possible, identified which piece or set of evidence was implicated in the quality control issue which arose. We then extracted an extensive description of the system malfunctions, failures, errors etc which together constituted the quality control failure which the detective reporting the case identified as his/her reason for reporting. Where further discussion of the case with the reporting detective revealed quality control issues of which s/he was initially unaware (because of his/her focus of interest) then these were also abstracted and recorded.

Finally the outcome of the case, the point at which a diagnosis of the issues was first made, and the involvement of formal supervisory procedures were all noted.

The second part of the analysis involves the assessments and personal characteristics of the reporting officer. We have asked why each case was reported, its perceived seriousness in quality control terms; whether the case engendered feelings of blame. We also wanted to give participants a chance to provide their own ideas about improving quality control. Inclusion of this second data set has allowed us to relate quality control attitudes, personal data and case experience in an attempt to account for some of the areas of variance.

We have used simple non-parametric (chi-square) measures of association to describe the internal structure of the data set. Where subsamples have been small, we have applied the appropriate small sample correction formulae (Norusis/SPSSinc 1990). Where these relationships are reported in the form "A is associated with B" no generalisation to all CID cases or all CID officers is implied. This study did not examine error in cases which went through the criminal justice system without incident. We have analysed a set of cases in which the quality control failures came to light and were reported to us. This caveat should be kept in mind when interpreting the statistical data.

THEORETICAL INTRODUCTION

Concepts and definitions

It has proved impossible to introduce this research without recourse to some special terms. Notably we have talked about the CID work system, about quality control, about system malfunctions and errors, human factors and quality control failures.

This simple systems language borrowed originally from engineering and incorporated into social science thinking in the 50's and 60's (eg. Trist et al 1963) provides a way of discussing in a relatively objective fashion, socio-technical phenomena which occur at work during processes of production. The product can be petroleum or CID case files, it matters not. Essential elements of the production system are merely inputs of various kinds, a series of interlinked transformations of those inputs, affected by a series of more or less known, more or less controllable forces, resulting in a series of outputs. By dint of feedback loops which put outputs back into the system as secondary inputs and by linking subsystems together in a variety of ways, this simple model can be elaborated ad infinitum.

The Social Sciences bolted on to this engineering model the idea of a social psychological system running in parallel with the engineering production system by virtue of having the mechanical bits of the production process manned rather than robotically controlled. The friction between the parallel social psychological and technical systems has been such that the history of production engineering has been characterised by the slow erosion of the power and influence of the manned side of the enterprise and the growth of robotic control.

The engine which has driven this historical development is quality control. Where objective measures have been taken of the factors tending to reduce the quality of production against established measurable criteria, human factors have been shown to account for most of the uncontrollable variance. This is simply because human operators do not perform repetitive production functions very accurately for long periods.

When systems thinking and concepts are applied to information processing rather than materials processing however, the human factors/ social system issues become more interesting. Human information processing is almost infinitely complex – capacity for judgement, discrimination, inference, projection, prediction, pattern recognition, pattern matching and a score of similar skills leave machines in the shade. However, these higher order skills are unfortunately even more sensitive to just the same kind of disruption by human factors as crude material processing tasks. Furthermore as the cognitive skills being practised in a system increase in complexity, so some of the effects of human factors (crudely of our humanity) become more subtle and difficult to detect.

To add to this complexity because higher order cognitive skills are essential to the ordering and functioning of social life, so social factors in the information processing work system affect outputs: the group can have an important impact on what we see, how we think, how we reason, what we attend to. Our role in the social group at work can also affect these things. So we face a paradox. In just those areas where our cognitive skills outgun machines, we are most vulnerable to our human and social nature. Moreover the effect of this vulnerability is difficult to detect and is often hidden by just the same exercise of skills: for example the mistake in reasoning caused by emotional upset will be hidden from view by a cover-up made possible by the human operator exercising his cognitive skills in his own defence.

Because information processing systems employ human beings at their most skilled, most valuable, most irreplaceable, defending such systems from human factors depredation has been a major task of engineering psychologists and other social scientists. System breakdown and quality control failure in such systems can have disastrous consequences. Most research has been generated by human factor problems in the armed forces, civil transport and the control of massive continuous process plants where control room operatives must manage highly complex incoming information.

Information processing systems of work come to the attention of human factors specialists as they start to create major concern either in terms of escalating cost or dangerousness or unreliability – or if high quality performance is especially important to the society in which such systems are operating.

It is the simple thesis of this study that a critical point has now been reached with the administration of criminal justice on several counts and that it is now therefore appropriate to start to apply systems thinking and human factors analysis to this system.

What are the general properties of the CID work system?

CID work has just been carefully investigated by Maguire (1992) with a view to proposing performance indicators. The picture drawn by Maguire and his colleagues does not differ in any marked way from that gleaned from 1979 field work for the Royal Commission in Criminal Procedure (Irving 1980). Indeed a number of commentators have pointed out that apart from some notable equipment, forensic and procedural changes, the essential ingredients of CID work have remained much the same for the last half century or more.

The preparation of cases against suspects (the end product of the system of investigation being a file) revolves around prime suspects . While investigations start with the gathering of relevant evidence, the aim of this preliminary process is to define one or more suspects. Once suspects have been identified by whatever method, investigative activity becomes more highly focused and the emphasis moves from putting someone "in the frame" to establishing a case against them which is sufficient to meet the current CPS test (that all other factors being equal there should be a realistic prospect of securing a conviction).

The sources of information for identifying suspects are in practice rather limited to the following of which the first two sources predominate (Burrows 1986):

- Eye witnesses, including victims' evidence particularly identifications or descriptions

- other witness evidence

- forensic or scenes of crime data from which identity or description can be inferred (including modus operandi)

- information provided by police informers

- information coming from surveillance, undercover or similar police activities whether new or held on criminal intelligence files

Witnesses can either be overt in that they come forward to offer obviously relevant information or they can be painstakingly uncovered by surveys, media memory jogging tactics etc. In many cases members of the public and patrolling police officers identify small behavioural or other variants from the normal flow of social life and these suspicious events are followed up not with a particular case in mind but on the off-chance that they will reveal criminal activity.

It is immediately apparent that looking for suspects involves some focused searching for and sifting of information but also an unfocused vigilance: a nose for the suspicious. In fact a divisional detective of some experience and skill will have his own case load for which he is responsible by himself or with others for focused information gathering and evaluation. But he will also be aware of a much wider case load so that he can make use of bits of information he comes across which do not fit his immediate set of "jigsaws".

If the through-put of cases in such a system was relatively small then the focused and unfocused activity could be carefully planned and monitored but the reality is that the average CID is deluged with cases and must select what to concentrate on.

Selection criteria are difficult to describe – there is an element of solvability, heinous crimes are always given priority and there may be a series of special drives in the force area against particular types of crime.

This sets the scene but it does not describe how the system works. Simply put, there is a unending supply of reported crimes allocated to CID officers by area and/or by crime type. Whatever the decision process, files land on individual desks and although team activities are constructed to deal with the exigencies of individual cases, the majority of case investigation work is handled by individuals and ad hoc teams of two or three officers loosely co-ordinated and nominally supervised by inspectors. In most instances detective sergeants can only be distinguished from detective constables by their experience and tendency to take the lead in the execution of activities.

As information gathering and processing gets more focused once suspects are identified and arrested, so files tend to revert to being the personal responsibility of the officer in the case.

Detective inspectors and chief inspectors are distanced from data gathering, recording and interpretation. They tend to be immersed in administering the department, coping with serious cases, special procedural or other problems, allocating work and planning and executing proactive CID initiatives such as surveillance, raids or special drives against particular crime. To keep going the department must rely heavily on the ability of individuals and small groups of DC's and DS's to organise themselves and deal with allocated cases as expeditiously as possible.

Before the advent of the Crown Prosecution Service, when the police prosecuted cases themselves or used in-house prosecution offices, as cases neared completion prosecutor and investigating officer tended to maintain a close relationship which was often criticised. The CPS solution devised by the RCCP has meant that the CID "product" now goes off to another agency for vetting. This has serious quality control repercussions.

While on the surface this work system seems to be akin to a research laboratory with small teams autonomously gathering, sifting and interpreting data, a major difference lies in the way the CID is set about with strict bureaucratic procedures. The case file becomes the material by which the CPS does its job in court. It is therefore not just the quality of the information processing, inference from data etc which is important, but the way in which all that work is meticulously recorded in a standardised way. Similarly in order to maintain criminal records and intelligence files, each case generates a series of reports, statistical forms and so on. The investigator may benefit from these databases indirectly, but emotionally detectives report that the paper work associated with cases feels like a separate clerical job. The satisfaction of being a detective can be glaringly at odds with officers' reactions to "the paperwork".

Returning briefly to the technology which is available to detectives to aid them in their tasks: scenes-of-crime departments, now largely civilianised, handle the search for and securing of physical evidence from scenes-of-crime. Forensic science laboratories, now operating as fee earning agencies, process forensic samples. The lead time for such processing can be considerable and cost and time constraints are important factors determining how CID's use forensic science services.

It is not common for Criminal Investigation Departments to be well supplied with personal computers or word processors and there are few if any tailored suites of software to aid the investigative process directly although a legal database is being trialed and the E-fit identification tool will soon be available in electronic form.

Cases often take detectives into situations which could be better understood with appropriate specialist knowledge. While experienced detectives either on special squads or in general CID work quickly acquire working knowledge of specialisms such as art, antiques, commercial procedures, drugs and mental health, expert advice in such matters is rarely on tap although working relationships with local universities and polytechnics are developing.

We can characterise the CID work system as comprising a number of simple stages:

- **1st**: search for suspect leads via available sources of information

- **2nd**: if possible identify and arrest suspects

- **3rd**: on the basis of available information and interview data from the suspect seek to construct an acceptable case sufficient to support a charge

- **4th**: if fail at stage three go round the loop again: or if partially successful seek to bolster the case with additional witness statements or other evidence

Like golf this is a deceptively simple game. The true complexity emerges when we go on to consider precisely what skills the detective has to deploy in order to:

- find a lead

- recognise it for what it is

- avoid missing relevant information

- extract valid and reliable information from suspects and witnesses

- draw valid conclusions from available data

- communicate accurately with colleagues about the above

- envisage what level of proof will be sufficient given little knowledge of the defence case

- use the available information to construct a case sufficient for court room purposes while not being expert in that system

- maintain accuracy of recording and communication in the face of heavy workload and bureaucratic demands

Such tasks are difficult enough in a benign environment. The operating environment of the modern urban detective is not benign.

To carry out these tasks effectively the detective deploys a number of cognitive skills. These skills are not equally developed in all individuals and within the same individual performance will vary with environmental, social, internal physiological and emotional states. Variation in skilled performance of the tasks imposed on detectives by work systems is the proper target of human factors research. Controlling that variance in a work system like that of the CID is often the best chance of improving quality of output if technological aids, bureaucratic procedures and the like are held constant. In this respect quality control is control of human factors.

Fundamentals of cognitive skill

Memory
Memory for a variety of identifiers is the detective's most salient mental tool. Until they acquire portable PC's updated daily from central intelligence files, CID officers will have to rely on their memory for faces, names, descriptions, addresses, aliases, methods of operation, known associates, telephone numbers, places of work – the list is endless.

The memorial capacity and efficiency of an experienced and competent detective is remarkable. However to understand that capacity, it is important to be a little more precise about the nature of memory.

There are two main ways in which memories are retained. Patterns of perception can be associated together and stick in memory as such (pictures, smells, the feel of things, sounds). Or items may be recorded in memory by virtue of their meaning – the way they logically or conceptually relate to other meaningful "ideas".

The more a memory is recalled and used, the more firmly embedded it becomes. But every usage adds a little to the memory: it becomes, by association with the way it is used each time, something slightly different.

In a darkened room alone, asked to recall strings of items, subjects perform rather badly – if the items learnt and then recalled have no meaning and no perceptual form, things get worse. Working memory for detectives is constantly being cued by their environment. They are "tipped off" by a sight or a sound or a word or a face or a number to recall the useful bit of information they have in memory.

However these tips or cues also affect how memories are recalled. So memorising and recalling is an active process in which new bits of information are created. It is not a passive mechanical process. (For an elegant discussion of memory in the Criminal Justice context see Loftus and Loftus 1976).

Perceptual discrimination and acuity
To say that detectives need to see and hear accurately and be able to discriminate effectively between different patterns of perceptual data seems obvious. But the ability to see the differences between two faces or hear the differences between two voices or recognise at a glance that two numbers on the page are slightly different, are underrated skills. Wine and tea tasters earn their living by exercising perceptual discrimination of a high order. In battle, aircraft spotting and radar watching are vital skills known to require special selection and training. Spotting a face in a crowd, recognising a voice from a taped surveillance exercise, spotting subtle changes in the fabric of every day life which are suspicious are the stuff of good detective work.

But again the perceptual apparatus as a whole is a creative, active system not mechanical. Sense data are sent to the brain down relatively neutral (mechanically acting) pathways. They are then interpreted and made meaningful by an active interface between memory and perceptual pathways. At this juncture individual memory can act to change what is seen and heard, felt and smelt both in subtle and even quite gross ways. (see Abercrombie 1960 for a condensed but classic account). The potential for this to happen is greater in naive than in trained observers but emotional, social and environmental conditions as well as the content of memory can

14

play havoc with human perceptual discrimination and acuity even among the trained. This happens not so much by virtue of what is perceived but how these sense data are interpreted and then communicated to others.

Vigilance and attention

Human perceptual and cognitive systems working normally fluctuate in efficiency through a diurnal 16 hour cycle before shutting down in sleep.

This operating period can be prolonged by high motivation or drugs but only with a consequent loss of operating efficiency when the effect wears off. If operatives are required to work in a way which runs counter to their established diurnal biorhythm, operating efficiency falls dramatically during what would be normal sleeping hours until a new pattern is established by the body. The ability to establish new patterns is variable – some people find it virtually impossible to adapt properly.

The main effect of loss of operating efficiency in the human perceptual and cognitive system is loss of vigilance in a task demanding it and an increasing inability to attend to any cognitive task which the individual faces. While extremes of motivation like fear of death in combat or sexual excitation or high levels of novelty in the operating environment can return attention and vigilance to normal levels for a time, this unnatural and heightened ability to attend is usually followed by complete collapse. This was the experience of using benzedrine to keep airborne troops going at the battle of Arnhem in World War II.

Loss of attention and vigilance in the performance of tasks like writing accounts of events, remembering data, processing information to reach inferences, interacting with others in a task, or making decisions, produces a rapid increase in all kinds of errors. If operatives are handling mechanical equipment then there is a heightened risk of accidents and malfunctions.

While these direct operational effects are well known to us all through personal experience, it is not so easy to appreciate the emotional effects of loss of attention and vigilance. Social relations depend on attention to cues about the others in the situation. Reading such cues allows the adaptation of behaviour to avoid over-aggressive or over-defensive reactions. With loss of attention and vigilance individuals acting in groups start to irritate and annoy each other, pathologies in group processes like leadership and co-operation quickly develop. These difficulties are often not properly ascribed and the effects on interpersonal relations can persist even when the individuals concerned have returned to their normal physiological state.

Reasoning

Under this heading fall a range of logico-deductive activities which are of central importance to the task of constructing a strong enough case against a suspect.

Having marshalled the available data as accurately as possible, investigators *always* face the problem of missing information, incomplete or unreliable information and misinformation (that is data which if taken as fact actively mislead).

Sifting what is available, filling in the gaps, shoring up the doubtful bits in an evidentiary chain requires the investigator to make logical inferences. It may be necessary to *deduce* that something is the case from a collection of relevant facts all pointing in that direction. Everyone gets around and performs socially by making deductions from available data. However in ordinary life there is a wide tolerance of error in the deductive process. We take a seat or a paper because it "appears" not to be owned – but the owner (if there is one) will correct us politely or not depending on a judgement about the degree and permissability of the error we are seen to have made in appropriating what is not ours. Legal proof requires that deductions be reliable beyond reasonable doubt. So wherever possible deductive reasoning is used as the basis for gathering further hard evidence that the reasoned deductive hypothesis is acceptable.

This process tends to set up an emotional push in the direction of the deduction. The deduction shapes the hypothesis – the hypothesis shapes the ensuing phase of the investigation. It follows that the nature of a detective's deductive reasoning is a crucial factor in determining the quality of the investigative process. So we shall consider reasoning skills in more detail.

There are some way stations between a set of data (evidence) and a deduction. In order to make deductions from data there are some simple techniques which start to develop in infancy and which are progressively refined in the process of cognitive development all the way up to their apotheosis as the main tools of scientific method.

Classification

It is a common mistake to confuse a neat arrangement of things which is pleasing in some way with a classification of items by one or more rules which define the classes into which items are placed or fall.

It is common practice for detectives to use time – space classifications for people so as to be able to determine logically who might have been physically able to commit a crime. Here the deductive principal is simple –

all suspects are classified on time and space dimensions; because a person cannot be at two different places at the same time, it follows that those distant from the crime scene at the relevant time cannot be suspect (unless!).

In such simple examples the classificatory skill lies in defining (unless). Obviously as we move into the field of high class detective work, classificatory schema and their use becomes rapidly more sophisticated: human remains of different ages scattered over a wide area; samples of a drug found on a number of people having some property in common are typical problems which may have to be tackled.

It would appear that some detectives carry simple classifications in their heads based on descriptions, methods of operation, recent activity, so that "ideas" about "who might be in the frame" develop rapidly by a not-fully-conscious logico-deductive process which nevertheless has considerable force. Classifications which are made on the basis of powerful rules can help us predict and fill in missing data by extrapolation. The accuracy of the prediction is proportional to the power of the rule. Thus Mendeleef, the classifier of the elements by atomic weight was able to predict the discovery of then unknown elements because of the power of the rule behind his classification.

Analogy
We carry rules about the relations between things and about their causation in our heads: they make rapid choice and action possible. Party games can be played with such visual illusions as holograms by hoodwinking subjects into "believing" in the solidity of mere light patterns. This is achieved by fulfilling all the main visual criteria for solidity and getting subjects to act quickly, not giving them a chance to bring tactile rules to bear. Detective work is full of working rules about causation, about suspicion and guilt, about patterns of behaviour and behavioural signatures. Many of these rules are not written down but are passed from experienced to inexperienced officers. The result is, as we would expect, that the same sort of people "come into the frame" for doing or being the same as previous generations of suspects. A new crime, or a new sort of suspect or a new method of operation takes time to work its way into the analogy repertoire.

Extracting rules from analogous previous material experience (the recording and recognition and utilisation of pattern) is probably the most wonderful, in the true sense of the word, attribute of human cognition. However it is a basic skill behind both art and science. It can be the basis for a creative act or, carefully constrained by a concern to be objective, it can be the basis of scientific prediction.

Working as they frequently do among deviant individuals in particular enclaves in society, detectives' analogies may be idiosyncratic and unreliable in certain ways. However users of analogies continually update their beliefs. If reasoning by analogy fails to produce a satisfactory result then the analogy is modified. Unfortunately the ability to modify the beliefs contained in analogies is variable. In extreme forms (neurosis) there is virtually no learning as a result of repeated failure, at the other extreme some people alter the belief systems on which they reason by analogy so rapidly and on such flimsy evidence, that their decisions are erratic and inconsistent.

Structured logic

The reasoning by analogy model described above appears to work in harness with a more structured rule-bound model of reasoning (Rips 1990). It would appear that some types of logical argument (eg. syllogisms) compel by their very structure and that human operators acquire a belief in these formal logical rules along with other looser self-generated beliefs. The rules of evidence provide detectives with one such model set of formal rules. Court precedent and legal experience define the kinds of reasoning and the level of proof likely to be accepted. This structured model of legal reasoning may or may not fit with the kind of loose rules by which detectives personally choose to reason by analogy.

Because reasoning depends on most of the other skills we have mentioned, it suffers additively from the problems that the exercise of all these other skills are prone to. It is just because of its centrality as a cognitive skill that reasoning ability is placed at the base of IQ assessment.

Decision and choice

The exercise of all cognitive skills involves some level of decision making. Remembering, recognising, discriminating, attending all involve the ability to choose between alternatives.

An example from the act of recognising a person will serve to illustrate the process at work. Someone faced with a recognition task has many faces, features, names and other identity details held in a web of complex associations in long term memory. Faced with a person in the field of vision, the recogniser is confronted with a task of comparing his memory store with what he sees, looking for a fit. Experimental evidence suggests that a decision to recognise is made when a fit occurs with a high enough subjective probability of being valid for the purposes for which the recognition is being made. In other words the recogniser assesses the cost of falsely recognising the person or failing to recognise him even though he knows him, against the benefit of currently recognising him. It follows that the criteria on which the judgement is made, depends on complex assessments of probabilities, costs and benefits of outcomes in the given situation. Needless to say these computations are always idiosyncratic – people divide rather neatly into optimists and pessimists in the computation of prob-abilities. It seems as though under- and over-assessment of costs and benefits in choice situations are also a matter of cognitive style. At a more general level a simple formal definition of the decision process runs as follows:

> "In making a decision it is thought that the individual chooses that action for which the sum of the probability of occurrence of the consequences multiplied by their utilities (taking into account the most positive and negative utilities) is the greatest." (Welford 1968)

It follows from this definition that if optimism or pessimism, or the computation of probabilities; or the prediction of consequences; or the definition of alternatives become too idiosyncratic (that is they become too far removed from what can objectively be shown to be the case) then decision making will begin to look irrational and unreliable. More impor-tant it will seem unpredictable and incomprehensible to others in a work group or system and will cause disruption and the ultimate breakdown of cooperative effort.

Communication

The skill which makes all work systems possible is communication – the ability to transfer the results of personal cognitive processing to others by sending verbal, written or signal messages. The process here involves the choice of an appropriate communication channel (write, speak, sign etc.); then encoding the message to be sent with due regard for:

- the characteristics of the channel

- the level of noise (interference) the message is likely to encounter

- the characteristics of the receiver

The receiver's task is to decode the message with the above in mind.

For our present purposes a few simple concepts from this complex field will suffice. All communication channels, have a finite capacity and a given efficiency. We talk of a radio being able to pick up a station. In reality this means that the signal from the station is strong enough, given the radio receiver's capacity (power) and efficiency to hear the signal against the sum of background noise, static etc.. A vital communication concept is therefore signal/noise ratio. With given channel capacity and efficiency as noise increases, hearing the signal, ie. receiving the communication depends on either increasing the amplitude of the signal pro rata or somehow increas-ing the efficiency of the receiver.

To overcome noise or the inefficiency of the channel or the inefficiency of the receiver, the transmitter can use amplitude (shouting) or redundancy (saying it over and over) or resort to multi-channel communication (writing it and saying it).

Encoding and decoding processes are again idiosyncratic within limits. These skills can be enhanced by appropriate training which is based on a full appreciation of how human communication systems work and break down. While it is easy to envisage increasing the amplitude of a message/signal by shouting, to do so by choice of words or enhancing words with pictures is a science in itself. The preferred legal communication modality is the spoken word in court (a notoriously difficult and socially divisive channel) and the document, or form, out of court. These two channels have very different characteristics and this in itself can lead to communication problems.

Because the investigative process generates more detail than the legal system can cope with, and because the trial process is a complex game (in the formal sense of this word; see Deutsch 1973) communication in the criminal justice process involves two fundamental sub processes – chunking and translation. Chunking occurs when detailed information is synthesised for transmission: the principle on which detail is condensed or left out will depend on the communicator's objectives, beliefs etc. Recently this sub process has come to notice via analysis of tape summaries (Baldwin 1991). He has demonstrated that this example of chunking has the same properties as other examples of the same phenomenon. That is, what is left out, or condensed, is often determined by the particular intentions and goals of the communicator.

Translation occurs when the communicator knows that the receiver at the other end of the channel is using some other language. Detectives translate their original messages for receipt by lawyers and court officials. While the translated message may be isomorphic with the original, that is not necessarily the case. This is equivalent to saying that something is always lost in translation. In this regard it is instructive to see how fast lawyers have, on the basis of "practicality", turned away from using either tapes of interviews or full transcriptions in favour of translations of chunked messages in the form of tape summaries. The need for translation also arises when inter-agency information is required. While agencies within the criminal justice system nominally all speak the same "language", investigations often involve other experts and professionals with their own distinctive languages. The most obvious examples are forensic scientists, psychologists, social workers and doctors.

The way in which messages are expressed in a given language depends to some extent on assumptions shared by sender and receiver.

These assumptions allow messages to be condensed – the level of redundancy can be reduced. This is why composing effective communication is easier among friends, close colleagues, or acquaintances – they share a common awareness of each others modes of expression. Where, in the course of investigations, detectives must switch from communicating inside the criminal justice system to communicating with outsiders, critical adjustments in the mode of expression may be necessary to maintain a given level of effectiveness.

What is quality and how can it be controlled?

In Maguire et al's discussion of CID performance indicators (Maguire, 1992), their CID informants are reported to value good quality detective work over any single measurement of their output such as the clear-up rate.

The search for performance indicators, developing as it has alongside police concerns about the quality of the service they provide, has led both the service and commentators on it into something of a philosophical quagmire. Quality is that attribute of a thing which expresses its worth in relation to some goal or objective. Because a goal or objective is very rarely unidimensional, and many of the dimensions are not measurable, the relevant judgements about worth may involve measurement but they always go beyond measurement into the arena of subjective and even political or aesthetic assessment.

Taking "good quality detective work" as a starting point, it is possible to see from Maguire's descriptions that the goal of detective work comprises:

- solving difficult-to-solve cases

- of relatively serious crime

- in such a way that the ensuing court room process moves efficiently towards an inevitable finding of guilt based on the results of the investigative process so as to make counsel and judge almost redundant

Quality detective work in this context is work likely to promote this goal. Put like this it is easy to see that quite small amounts of error in the preparation of a case can produce disproportionate reductions in the probability that a case will conform to the ideal. All the characteristics of "good quality detective work" imply that the investigator must be operating at full stretch to produce a seamless web of evidence in a difficult case. Likewise many cases in which no error is made and which at certain points appear to conform to the ideal are actually non-contenders because they offer no real challenge and do not bring detective skills properly into play.

Here lies a difficulty: if cases where the chance of demonstrating quality detective work are quite rare and yet in these the quality can be easily spoilt by small errors or skill decrements, then how do detectives keep up the quality of their output as they tend to define it? Do they have dual goals and hence dual definitions of quality and switch from one to the other or do they try and maintain the same standards and definitions throughout their work?

Legal philosophy formally binds the CID to one set of standards – it is not legally or politically acceptable that the quality of investigation shall be differently defined for a minor burglary and for a murder. But this legal *force majeure* does not make the problem go away. In reality there are many definitions of quality around both at a departmental and at an individual level, but as Maguire has argued there is a clear consensus on some of the issues – that is detectives can tell you which are quality cases and which are not.

Outsiders can of course pitch in with their own definitions. Quality can be defined from the point of view of the economy or the victim or the court. However the aim of this study is to concentrate on detective skills and what affects the exercise of them. We are therefore bound to go for an internal definition of quality of some kind. We can roughly define the tasks that detectives have to do and the skills they have to bring to bear. What we do not have are any firm quality control criteria – that is rules by which we can judge when the skilled performance of a detective in a given case falls to such a level that the quality of that CID output can be said to have failed the test.

The nature of controls

In serious cases at least finding suspects, constructing a proof, getting admissions, running informers, using criminal intelligence are craft skills involving, as we have described, higher order cognitive skills. Alongside the craft part of the CID job runs the clerical and administrative stream of forms and procedures. The latter is the record of the former but it does not contain it. In routine cases the administrative tasks outweigh all others.

The definition of quality in a clerical system is relatively easy:

- forms must completed accurately in the right order

- procedures must be completed in a timely and accurate way

- information must be transmitted through the prescribed network as stipulated

It follows that process and data checking machinery is likely to be available in most clerical systems to ensure that documents are compiled, collated and transmitted properly. But what of the craft output – the essence of the work from the detectives' point of view?

In traditional craft based production systems, the quality control responsibility for the exercise of craft skills lies with the craftsman himself. For that reason the apprenticeship is long and arduous. The role of the craft foreman is heavily circumscribed: he may point out the failure of the individual to perform in such a way that his output can be combined with that of his workmates: he may seek to adjust speed of output and he certainly has the authority to take action if the craftsman's own quality controls fail. However he does not interfere with the manner in which the craft skills are exercised. As long as the craft product is acceptable to the next stage of production, then the craft foreman protects the autonomy of the craftsman; may even be said to collude with it.

There are strong echoes of this arrangement in the CID. However there are also massive differences in the operating environment which make the similarities a matter of concern.

The CID apprenticeship is not long and arduous. It is less so now than it was although the number of reported crimes is self-evidently higher and rising and the falling clear-up rate suggests that in general the task of the detective is getting harder.

The output (the case file) is not a given with measurable and immutable characteristics, it is an organic entity: a bundle of more or less reliable facts and propositions which will be changed radically as it moves through the system. Moreover the detective will be asked to continue his involvement with this output as it goes forward.

The CID production system is open to other systems all of which impact on the work of the detective: the CID is not a factory. The CID product, being organic in character, does not have a fixed, known or predictable use in court as for example an engine block has in an engine; so the detective is always uncertain as to the tolerances he is working to.

We would argue that under these circumstances neither a clerical checking nor a craft quality control system are by themselves or in combination adequate.

The need for organising principles

Normal operation in an organic system produces sameness, regularity and consistency. By contrast pathology and malfunctions produce unique kinds of distortion.

The quality control failures brought to us by detectives bear out this principle in that unlike the "normal" run of cases, each one has very particular features usually clustered around the points in the process of investigation where things went wrong. It has been important not to get bogged down in these unique features; we have therefore used a limited number of heuristics to organise the data in what we believe will be a helpful way.

First we have concentrated on the evidentiary point where the quality control failure occurred in order to answer the question-in what particular did this case go wrong for this investigator who reported it? The second heuristic has been more problematic: we needed to classify types of quality failure in such a way that, without jumping to conclusions, we could judge what human factors issues were relevant and get some indication of their relative importance. The difficulty arises because in some cases there is clear evidence of what kind of skilled performance went wrong, while in others no such indications exist and inferences have to be made on the basis of incomplete data. In order to make the inferential process as clear as possible, we have initially classified quality control failures by the task activity involved. A given case with failures at a number of evidentiary points can involve several different tasks – activities that went wrong. Most of these defined tasks or activities involve a known set of skills – so even if we cannot say precisely what went wrong, we can, at the next level of generality, identify what human factors are most likely to have been implicated. An example may help to clarify this point. A case is reported because in court a police eye-witness fails to convince: the police statement is the focus of the problem, it is ambiguous. At court the quality of the written statement destroys the credibility of the officer. The quality control failure is the written eye-witness account. Although we do not have specific indications of what went wrong with the skilled performance – writing an eye-witness account – we are aware of the skills involved in that process and how they are affected by internal and external factors. In another case based on a similar issue, the evidence is better, the informant diagnoses the situation himself saying he was emotionally overwrought; it was 2.00 am when he wrote the account and his memory and communication skills were duly impaired.

The classification of human factor causes of quality control failure

Anyone who has had to listen to excuses or explanations as to why accidents have occurred will know that they are infinitely variable in their detail. The brief discussion of cognitive skills and the way they are used in detective work introduced the notion that wherever cognitive skilled performance is in train then there are a wide diversity of ways in which that skilled performance can be knocked off course.

Almost anything can put us off our cognitive stroke. However this looming complexity can be very substantially simplified. All skilled human performance requires an optimum state of neurophysiological arousal to maintain the best average output that the operator is capable of. If, for whatever reason, arousal falls too low (boredom, inattention, drowsiness etc) or rises too high (over excitement, anxiety, distress etc) then performance rapidly falls off. At the extremes, errors and malfunctions become common. (This general principle is known as the Yerkes Dodson law [Yerkes and Dodson 1908]). The individual has a built in gyroscope which self-corrects arousal within fairly narrow limits but this is a widely varying ability – the depressed cannot raise their arousal level at all, the manic cannot reduce it.

Every job has its sources of over- and under-arousal and it is the task of the ergonomic consultant to identify them and cope with controllable factors such as design of equipment, heat, light, ventilation, crowding, toilet and canteen facilities – all the things that worry human operators (Galer 1987). Similarly it is the task of managers and job designers to ensure that people are not underaroused at work.

While no such ergonomic analysis of detective work in available, we do have a great deal of data on police stress and its causes. In essence this is the same thing because reported stress derives from chronic over- and under-arousal. We can therefore use findings in the stress field to identify the most likely causes of the kind of over- and under-arousal which also cause quality control failures. The stress research studies provide a useful organising principle for considering the causes of quality control failure.

Moreover because police stress factors have been identified and even ranked in importance (Alexander et al 1991), we can use these findings and the theoretical position described above as a check on our analysis and the classification of the quality control failures brought to us. The sources of errors in the case histories should fit the classification of stress factors.

A working classification of police stress factors

Davidson's (1980) review of stress factors (in Cooper and Marshall 1980) relies heavily on American research on the police. However, the classification of factors constructed by the author from the American data has since been validated in an occupational health audit of a UK force (see Alexander et al 1991). We shall therefore adopt this classification. Davidson fits the specific sources of police stress identified in the literature into the general typology developed by Cooper and Marshall (1976) and Davidson and Veno (1977).

- Factors intrinsic to a particular job

- Factors relating to role in the organisation

- Factors linked to career development

- Relationships at work

- Organisational structure and climate

The specific issues mentioned under each of these headings are as follows:

Factors Intrinsic to the Job:

a. Equipment: failure of equipment either due to poor design, poor state of repair or insufficient operator training. Much equipment is used infrequently and only in emergencies. Other equipment like cars are used so heavily that adequate servicing becomes a problem.

b. Shiftwork: stresses associated with being on a particular shift or changing from one shift to another. Family and social life can produce stress around a particular shift which is not in itself stressful. The management of the shift system can produce stressful inequities.

c. Job overload/underload: the variable and uncontrollable nature of the inputs to the CID work system means that occasional overload is an integral part of the job. By the same token periods of overload may be followed by slack periods when boredom becomes a problem.

d. Courts: police officers operating in an alien context, sometimes without much experience or relevant training; they can feel on trial themselves. Scheduling of appearances demonstrates lack of concern for their priorities and their status.

e. Physical danger/emotional involvement: danger and involvement in heinous crimes promote over arousal, as does facing circumstances which are personally dangerous.

Role in the Organisation:

a. Ambiguities in the police role: crime prevention versus detection – enforcement versus service.

b. Conflict between police roles e.g. bureaucrat versus crime fighter

c. Conflict between the policing role and the community represented by either specific roles or institutions. Conflict between the policing role as seen by the police and as seen by the community.

Career Development

a. Over- and under-promotion

b. Frustrations created by thwarted ambition etc

c. Adequacy of training for present job

Relationships at Work

a. Work group relations

b. Superior/subordinate relations

c. Relations with other work groups, specialisms etc

Organisational Structure and Climate

a. Office politics

b. Sink or swim, macho management techniques accompanied by inadequate training and supervisory support

c. Lack of consultation and participation in management decisions

d. Quality and appropriateness of administration/over-bureaucratisation

e. The discipline system and the nature of informal sanctions

Examples taken from the case histories under each of these headings are described later in the report.

FINDINGS

Limitations of the methodology

The accounts we have been able to collect of cases which, in the eyes of investigators, are quality control failures, have been largely aural without documentary back-up. Checking the files for each case has allowed us to validate the main structure of cases and events within them but the accounts have for obvious reasons not been recorded on file.

Where the important issues came to light in Crown court they would be a matter of record but this would only apply to very few cases. The exact circumstances in which each particular problem arose are therefore only available in the collective memories of those intimately involved. We are limited in the extent to which we can unravel causation under these circumstances. We have to rely on what our informants remember and even then they can only supply what they themselves have direct knowledge of. Some of our case histories are more complete than others. This is so particularly in terms of the fine detail around the exact point at which a problem developed.

We have therefore resorted to describing the sample of cases as precisely as we can in categoric terms which can be fleshed out with qualitative detail from the case histories where the coded descriptions fail to capture the essence of the data.

In the time available we have had limited access to each informant to obtain their subjective reaction to the case history they produced. While this subjective data helps to round out case histories, we have had to be careful not to fall into the trap of pushing investigators into attempting to establish the causations of their own actions. On the other hand where detailed and plausible explanations have been offered without prompting and have clear psychological validity then we have treated that data as potentially valuable. In this category would fall those instances where investigators have acknowledged tiredness, overload, emotional involvement in the outcome of cases and reckless decisions to ignore the possible consequences of procedural rules.

Summary negative findings

This study was proposed in the first place because it appeared that the CID work system had never been subjected to any kind of ergonomic analysis and that therefore no empirically based quality control system was operating.

It follows from this original stance that the more formalised null hypothesis for the study would be something along the following lines:

The sources of human error in the CID work system are well known and described and all reasonable and practicable steps are taken in training, supervision and the design of practices and procedures to avoid such errors becoming the possible sources of miscarriages of justice.

Before dealing in detail with the findings it will simplify reporting to deal with some aspects of this null hypothesis in a summary manner.

A. *The Sources of Human Error in the CID Work System are Well Known and Described*

There is no evidence in any of the interviews that have been conducted for this study that this is the case. The informants have been mostly experienced officers yet they have not used any standardised descriptions of the quality control problems they have encountered. Indeed they have often needed to talk to the researcher for some time about general issues in order to get the point of the study. There has been no evidence of any formal or informal vocabulary having developed to deal with the phenomena that have been described to us.

On this negative evidence it would be dangerous to accept the null hypothesis in respect of proposition A.

B. *During Training all Reasonable Steps are Taken to Teach Police Officers how to Avoid the Errors to which CID Work is Prone*

The conclusion of the training review (q.v.) is as follows. With very limited exceptions in training modules relating to work with vulnerable people (with respect to the Police and Criminal Evidence Act (PACE)), and dealing with identification problems, police officers are not directly taught about their own fallibility as information processors. They are not told what particular errors to look out for nor are they instructed when those errors are likely to manifest themselves. There are no direct explanations of linkages between supervisory or documentary procedures and the need to avoid certain types of error. So supervisory procedures are not generally perceived as there to help the officer control the quality of work or enhance overall performance.

Management and supervisory courses do not have any ergonomic content. Supervisors are not given a systems view of the work they are supervising. In general they are taught to make sure that the mechanics of the system operate as prescribed: the inevitable malfunctions in such systems are not explained nor are there any direct efforts made to help supervisors plan and deal with the constant threat and reality of such malfunctions. Indeed it would appear that where supervisory training does touch on such matters, the personal responsibility view is paramount and discussion of the issues shades into the management of the discipline system, the sanctions available against officers, and morale and leadership issues. We do not intend to denigrate or belittle this approach only to point out that what should be a complementary attention to the systems issues we have outlined is notably missing. Again on the evidence we have to reject this part of the null hypothesis.

C. Supervisory Practice and Procedure

There is virtually no evidence on the relevant case files or supporting documentation of the problems and issues brought to us during this study. We are therefore dealing almost entirely with aural evidence which has been provided by operational detectives. In the vast majority of cases, the evidence comes from investigating officers not supervisors who are often unaware of the case if the problems therein have been contained by the investigating officer. Supervisors only come into the picture when a team investigative effort is concerned and they are aware of the issues because of their close operational support of the case. This is no more than saying that all the evidence of human factors issues which has been passed to us has come from very close to the seat of operations: these data do not appear to percolate any distance up the hierarchy unless something goes badly wrong, there are complaints from other agencies, or a disciplinary procedure comes into play.

It follows that there can be no synthesis of relevant data, no ongoing checking of procedures in any systematic way. Such quality control checking depends on the existence of appropriate management information systems. Not only are these not available but the current CID culture would tend to militate against their evolution. The null hypothesis is also rejected on this count.

Findings from the sample of case histories

The Sample of Cases

Sixty case histories have been collected and analysed. The main informant associated with each reported case has been interviewed to obtain background information, personal characteristics and attitudes.

The sample of cases contains a subset of cases identified by the Crown Prosecution Service rather than the police (n = 12). Local officers of the CPS were asked to identify cases on the same criteria as police officers. This was done to provide a check in the quota sample provided by the police. Had any serious censorship occured, we reasoned, CPS employees would report to us cases which would otherwise have been concealed.

However, a comparison does not suggest any attempt at censorship. These cases do not differ in any marked respect from those reported by police officers. If anything the CPS cases are slightly less likely to be serious and are more likely to involve problems with witnesses "both police and other". There is no evidence that the Crown Prosecution Service are identifying issues of which the police are either unaware or which they are in some way seeking to conceal from the research. Indeed the findings will show that officers have been completely frank about all kinds of issues up to and including breaches of Police and Criminal Evidence Act rules.

For the purposes of this analysis therefore we see no reason to treat the two subsets of data separately.

Type of Crime and Crime Seriousness

The types of crime involved in the case histories have been grouped as indicated below:

The distribution of cases in the sample is as follows:–

Table 1
The distribution of cases in the sample according to crime type

Type of Crime	%	N (60)
• all property crime except those with an element of violence either during the crime or at arrest	45	27
• other property crimes with an element of violence	13	8
• crimes against the person including sexual crimes	27	16
• fraud	3	2
• drugs	8	5
• public order	3	2

Cases were divided into serious and non-serious not on any strict legal definition but rather according to the circumstances of the case as seen from the investigators' view point. Thus if a complex drug surveillance operation yielded a legally trivial charge, that case would still be classified as serious. However, in general property crimes under £100.00 were classed as not serious; crimes against the person involving ABH or common assault were treated as not serious; GBH, wounding and serious sexual assaults were classed as serious. Any case involving multiple charges was classified by its most serious charge. In all 65% of cases were classed as serious. (N=39)

Types of Evidence Implicated in the Cases

Each case history involved a range of types of evidence. Only some of the available evidence tended to be implicated in the problem which had

31

caused the officer in the case to bring it to our attention. In order to see what kinds of data are most frequently implicated in quality control failures and in what way, a typology of evidence was produced and each case history was analysed to identify which types were implicated.

The following table describes each type of evidence and the frequency with which it is implicated in quality control issues over the sample as a whole. The types are presented in rank order by frequency.

Table 2
Types of evidence implicated in the cases

Evidence Type	% of case histories where implicated	N (60)
Police statements (general)	37	23
Statements by independent witnesses	30	18
Admission statement by suspect	23	14
Police statement (of identification)	25	15
Real evidence (other than documentary)	23	14
Documentary evidence	22	13
Statements by victims (excluding identifications)	17	10
Identifications by independent witnesses	15	9
Forensic evidence (chemical, biological, fingerprints)	13	8
Identifications by victims	15	9
Other expert evidence	12	7
Forensic psychological evidence	7	4
Evidence from identification parades and other forms of ID validation	2*	1

* In most cases involving identification it is the *absence* of ID validation procedures which caused the problems.

The distribution indicates that quality control issues implicate a wide range of types of evidence. While there are cases in which a number of types of evidence are implicated in the quality control issue, the majority are affected by a single difficulty although that one difficulty can have very far reaching repercussions. In 67% (N=40) of the cases a single type of evidence is implicated. In 20% (N=12) there are two types and in 14% (N=8) more than two.

Types of Quality Control Issue

In order to overcome the particularity with which things go wrong, our main analytic task has been to arrive at a working classification of types of quality control issue. There are many such classifications which could be tried. The one reported here has been constructed inductively after a careful reading of all the case histories with an eye to trying to capture the issues most salient to the Royal Commission's work. It is in two parts. **Part A** deals with domains of error: that is errors are classified by where in the process they become manifest. **Part B** classifies error by manifest cause. This is a difficult but important distinction. The investigator's job involves conforming to a number of rules and procedures so that the resulting case stands up in court. Specific failures, regardless of cause, in any of these areas produces a predictable impact on the case's progress through the system (assuming the error comes to light).

On the other hand a case can go astray not at a defined point in the process of investigation when a given procedure or rule is breached, but because of a specific error in the way in which a particular task is performed by the investigator so that it has a knock-on or cumulative effect on the investigative process as a whole. Both types of error may occur in the same case. It will be only too apparent that we have not included in part B of the classification such obvious "causes" of error as expediency, laziness, greed etc. (i.e. moral turpitude). This is because, not surprisingly, our informants did not present their case histories to us in this way. Where it was evident that a rule had been deliberately broken for expedient reasons, our informants inevitably said that they had failed to properly reason out the consequences of their actions.

For those who feel that plain badness should not be left out of the aeteology of criminal justice errors, category 11 below is the most relevant. The quality control failures which fall into this category are bound to be the result of a mixture of true failures to perceive consequences correctly and unwillingness to recognise them in the face of more pressing personal motivation.

In the current climate of concern about police ethics it is important to emphasise that this research cannot embrace cases where the investigating officer choses to breach rules and procedures, is aware of the probable consequences but either gets away with it or is unconcerned by what subsequently happens. Likewise, we were not likely to come across cases in which breaches of rules and procedures were genuinely the result of lack of awareness of possible consequences and there was no subsequent denouement so that officers remained unaware.

Each class of quality control issue is discussed below with examples, and a frequency table is given showing the relative importance of each error type in this sample of cases.

A. Domains of Error
1. Errors in the administration of the Police and Criminal Evidence Act
The Police and Criminal Evidence Act and accompanying codes lay down a considerable number of procedures to which investigating and custody officers and their superiors must adhere. Officers are liable to error:–

- in carrying out the procedures

- in recording that the procedure has been carried out

- in interpreting whether or not or how the procedures apply

We have distinguished carefully between unconscious errors in these categories and direct breaches of procedural rules (see below).

2. Breaches of Police and Criminal Evidence Act rules

Apart from prescribing certain procedures, the PACE Act creates a number of procedural rules. On occasion these rules are breached more or less consciously. The motivation for such breaches can range from pressure of work to the feeling that justice would be better served by the breaches than the observance. We feel it right to distinguish between errors in managing the PACE Act procedures and rule breaches because the quality control implications are quite different: improving quality in the latter case involves dealing with the motivation issues whereas specific motivation is not relevant to minimising the errors subsumed under the first heading. Breaches still involve errors in that the rule breaker invariably makes some error of judgement in coming to a decision to break the rules. It is the error of judgement with which this research is concerned not the impropriety.

3. Errors in managing vulnerable suspects under the PACE Act

Because there are particular concerns about the management of vulnerable suspects in the criminal justice system, we have specifically identified cases where procedural errors stopping short of breaches of rules have occurred in relation to the mentally ill, handicapped etc.

4. Breaches of PACE Act rules in relation to vulnerable suspects

For the same reason we have also identified cases where specific rules relating to the management of vulnerable suspects have been breached.

5. Error by an expert witness

The complexity of modern work systems and the proliferation of professions means that many more expert witnesses are now called to give evidence. These experts are not necessarily trained as witnesses: in presenting their evidence and in communicating with the police they can mislead and on occasion make errors either in interpreting their data or in presenting facts. Because there is a current debate about the status and quality control of expert evidence, we have identified errors associated with expert witnesses as a special class.

6. Error through false attribution of expert status by the police to a witness or informer

As the world in which investigators operate becomes more complex, so the need to obtain independent expert help from outsiders during investigations is bound to rise. Those who appear to be expert may of course not be so: they may merely want to be helpful or they may have ulterior motives for giving their opinions.

We have distinguished between cases where difficulties arose with experts who could reasonably be described as such and cases involving people who were attributed with expert status by the police on plausible but insufficient grounds. In all cases this false attribution arose because of a tendency to overvalue certain administrative roles and ascribe professional levels of technical knowledge to them.

7. Legal errors

It seems that the English criminal law is complex enough for errors of fact and interpretation to plague all those who have to work with it on a daily basis. The police make errors; so do the CPS, magistrates and their clerks, and even Crown Court judges.

8. Apparent divergence from normal CID/force procedure

There are standard procedures for dealing with most eventualities in the investigation of crime. Standing orders and the content of training are aimed at getting things done in a way which will produce reliable and sufficient evidence in court. Because many of these procedural prescriptions are intended to safeguard the system, they can often be long-winded and irksome. We have found that in many instances whatever else has caused a quality control failure in a given case, it is also clear that a normal procedure had been by-passed, fore-shortened or not properly completed. In these cases the solution cannot be to implement a procedure – there already is one. We have introduced this class of quality control issue to distinguish between cases where the problem lies with a failure to apply an existing procedure and cases where no existing procedure appears relevant.

9. Problems of continuity of evidence

Preparing a case for trial requires the investigating officers to so arrange their evidence that a causal chain connecting the suspect to the offence is established. When there seems to be very strong grounds for suspecting someone of a crime, gaps in this chain can go unnoticed. While the lapses in reasoning and acuity which allow this to happen belong in section B below, continuity of evidence is an important domain in which errors occur.

10. The contamination of forensic evidence

For forensic scientists to do their job properly, the evidence needs to be carefully collected, packaged, labelled etc. Sometimes errors are made at this stage because investigators or other officers are not fully alive to the effect their actions can have on forensic science investigation.

B. Causes of Error

11. Deductive reasoning – perceiving consequences and estimating risk

Because investigating officers are preparing cases for court partially unaware of what the defence will say or how witnesses will perform (including themselves) the ability to foresee the consequences of investigative decisions and second guess the defence are important reasoning skills. It is clear from the case histories that if either the case does not seem worth the trouble, or if everything about it seems cut and dried, the effort to foresee how the case will develop is not made and sometimes unforeseen circumstances can supervene with serious consequences. We have distinguished between instances where sufficient information to make appropriate deductions was available and those where it was not.

12. Quality of information processing

At base all instances of quality control failure involve some human information processing error but because of the constraints under which we are working, it has not been possible to trace the full aetiology of each quality control issue brought to us. In this class we have recorded all the cases where we have direct evidence of causes of information processing error.

13. Communications issues

The effective preparation of cases and bringing them to court successfully depends on communication at a number of levels. We have coded breakdown in communication by level from individual to agency. Because the shift system and the complexity of arrangements for various kinds of duty including training means that officers are often absent in an unpredictable way, some communication problems are specifically the result of absences from work. We have coded this problem separately.

The Incidence of Error Types in the Sample of Cases

Cases have been classed under more than one heading in the table below. Not all cases are coded under B because it was not always possible to ascertain causes.

Table 3
Domains of error

A. Domains of error	%	N (60)
1. Errors in the administration of the PACE Act	30	18
2. Breaches of PACE rules	22	13
3. Errors in managing vulnerable suspect under the PACE Act (excluding breaches of rules)	7	4
4. Breaches of PACE Act rules re vulnerable suspect	3	2
5. Errors by acknowledged expert	8	5
6. Errors by pseudo-experts	10	6
7. Legal errors:		
police	8	5
CPS	8	5
courts	7	4
8. Divergence from CID procedure	53	32
9. Continuity of evidence problems	28	17
10. Contamination of forensic evidence	8	5

Table 4
Causes of error

B. Causes of error	%	N (60)
11. Deductive reasoning – foreseeing consequences		
information sufficient	30	18
information insufficient	12	7
12. Quality of information processing	40	24
13. Communication		
Inter person	7	4
Inter department	5	3
Inter force	4	2
Inter agency	32	19
14. Communication failure caused by the absence of at least one party	15	9

The most common domains of error are therefore:

- the PACE Act

- divergence from CID procedure

- continuity of evidence

The most common causes of error are:

- failure to deduce that certain consequences damaging to a case will occur as a result of decisions taken

- information processing

- failures of communication between CID and external agencies (notably CPS and the courts)

The Diagnosis of Quality Control Failure

In general most quality control failures are spotted by the skilled operative as they occur. In typical work systems layers of supervision and quality control produce diminishing returns in terms of errors detected.

To check whether the administration of criminal justice conforms to this general pattern, the cases in the sample were checked to see at what point the errors involved came to light.

The following distribution of diagnosis over the stated detection points was observed:

Table 5
Distribution of diagnosis

	%	N
The investigating officer himself	15	9
CID supervisor	12	7
Crown Prosecution Service	18	11
In court (as a result of trial process)	54	32

These findings are the opposite of the typical quality control system result. The reasons for this pattern of diagnosis are embedded in the sorts of error which are made. Breaches of established procedure will tend to be either concealed or will not be expected in a work system where operatives are responsible for their own output and there are serious sanctions against breaches of the rules. Likewise failure to foresee the consequences of investigative decisions can only be diagnosed by a supervisor with equal knowledge of the case and superior reasoning ability: there is no reason why, given the way the system works, any CID supervisor should be currently providing that kind of quality control. Failures of communication in messages going outward from the CID to other agencies or coming inward to the CID from outside cannot, in the worst cases, be diagnosed as such until the various parties to the process come together in court to test the case. It is thus that our current criminal justice system places upon the court room process a major responsibility not only for trying cases but for testing the quality of the investigative process which has led up to the trial.

This, of course, would not necessarily be problematic if the trial was not an adversarial affair in which attempts to discover the other side's errors goes hand in hand with trying to minimise the impact of one's own.

In a number of cases brought to us in this study the officers involved have been worried by what has happened but are content that the likelihood of the full story coming out in court is minimal. In all these cases the shape of the evidence generally suggests that this failure of the trial process to diagnose the error will ensure that a guilty person is convicted and does not get off on a technicality, but there is no way of being sure. Any one of the errors implicated in these case histories could, under the right circumstances, help secure a false conviction just as easily as a false acquittal. Although as we shall see below it is alleged false acquittals that predominate in our sample.

Outcomes

Table 6
Outcomes

	%	N
Guilty	17	10
Not guilty	20	12
Not guilty on direction	12	7
Case dismissed	12	7
Case withdrawn	22	13
Other (no charge etc)	2	1
Not known	15	9

Although it is perhaps presumptuous to have done so, we have tried to estimate from the files and case histories whether the quality control failures had the effect of increasing the likelihood of a false conviction or a false acquittal. In 65% (N=39) of cases there was insufficient data to make the judgement. In 28% (N=17) it appeared on balance that the problem had increased the likelihood of a false acquittal and in about 4 cases the likelihood of false conviction seems to have been increased. However, in none of these cases had a guilty verdict actually been recorded, whereas all the "false acquittal" cases had actually ended in acquittal. Again, however we have to re-emphasise that there was nothing about any of the errors in the false acquittal group of cases which meant that they could not have had the opposite effect in different circumstances. Also these judgements were made on the basis of police files and police accounts.

Of the 16 cases in which an error was made in the application of PACE Act rules and procedures, 5 were classified as possible false acquittals.

Of the 11 cases where PACE Act rules were broken, 4 were classed as possible false acquittals.

Of the 4 cases in which errors were made with the management of vulnerable suspects under the PACE Act, 2 were classed as possible false acquittals.

Of the 31 cases in which CID procedures were not properly followed, 6 cases were classified as possible false acquittals.

The 4 cases which appeared to be heading for a false conviction before the errors were discovered did not involve the PACE Act in any way.

We have been struck by the way in which police investigative errors coming to light in court have been dealt with. while it may be the fact that judges and magistrates are not meant to use the dismissal of cases as a means or opportunity to criticise the police that is how it often comes across to investigating officers.

Sometimes the issue upon which a dismissal is based is a matter of organisation and management: equipment may not be available to view evidence, people may not be present, documents may be missing. Dismissals which follow upon such organisational and managerial errors, not always of the police's making, create serious disaffections between police, lawyers and officers of the court. This disaffection is quite clear in relevant case histories in our sample. Its effect, we believe, is to destroy the motivation necessary for police to maintain high standards of case preparation.

A final outcome measure which we have coded because it has leapt at us from the case histories was whether or not the quality control failures observed lead to aspersions being cast in court on the probity of the police. Sometimes attacking police probity is part of defence strategy but it feeds on quality control lapses.

In 35% (N=21) of the cases in the sample aspersions were cast on police probity in court as a result of or at least contingent upon quality control difficulties which arose. Allegations included the fabrication of evidence, the alteration of statements to make them more probative, cynically breaking PACE Act rules to obtain confessions and offering suspects deals. In all the cases which we have analysed, save one, the allegations made in court by the defence on the basis of the error made in the case, were more severely critical of police behaviour than the error seemed to us to warrant when seen in context. Nevertheless, these exaggerated inferences could not easily be rebutted because in most cases early diagnoses of the errors were not made, and even where they were made, the details of what had happened were not recorded on file or talked through with supervisors. We have already argued that this study does not deal with "badness", only with error. Quite clearly a number of breaches of the PACE Act reported to us were deliberate but the subsequent decision of the officers concerned to collaborate with this research was based in the main on recognition of their own poor judgement or deductive reasoning.

There would seem to be considerable scope for making investigating officers more actively aware of the reasons for the rules they are asked to keep and the likely consequences of breaking them regardless of whether these consequences come to light or affect them directly. It is awareness of the consequences of breaking ethical and legal rules which lies at the basis of practical ethics and not mere knowledge that rules and procedures exist.

Types of Crime, Evidence and Quality Control: do Certain Crimes Tend to Produce Certain Kinds of Quality Control Problem?

Before proceeding to look at associations between these variables the limitations of our methodology need underlining. Because we have not taken a random sample of cases or a random sample of error making activity we cannot generalise about these populations. We are considering this particular quota sample because we think, given the time and resources available, its characteristics are more likely to shed light on the making of errors in the investigative process than anything else we could study. The statistics quoted are descriptions of the sample only. They do not imply an unwarranted attempt to generalise.

Crime type and evidence

In general there are no strong associations between type of crime and the type of evidence implicated in the quality control problem which led to cases being reported to us. While we have to be careful not to accept associations too readily on the basis of the small numbers in each class, the following observed biases are plausible:

- In property crimes there is a tendency for police statements to be a source of difficulty

- In crimes against the person there is a preponderance of identification statement issues, usually involving problems of validation

- Admission statements are at issue in 25% of cases overall but in half of crimes against the person.

These biases are not strong enough to suggest that in this sample certain types of crime determine what kinds of evidence will be implicated in any subsequent quality control issue. As we shall see it is the type of activity which affects what kind of error is made and activities in the investigative process tend to be much the same in very different types of crime.

41

Crime seriousness and evidence

More serious crimes are likely to put more pressure on the police, on forensic services and expert witnesses. As might be expected the serious cases tend to implicate proportionately more police statements and police identifications in subsequent quality control problems. Serious cases also involve more problematic psychological and expert testimony than non-serious cases. However, this bias does not apply to general forensic evidence or admission statements which are equally likely to play a part in serious and non-serious cases.

Somewhat surprisingly, while evidence type and crime seriousness are related, there is no association between crime seriousness and the classification of types of quality control problem we have created. Problems of continuity of evidence, quality of information processing, errors in the administration of the PACE Act procedures etc. are just as likely to occur in the trivial as in the serious cases. The tasks involved in proving a case against someone who steals a trivial amount are not intrinsically different from those involved in dealing with a very serious theft. It is the nature of the activity and the conditions in which that activity takes place which hold the key to the likelihood of error and which determine what kind of error will be made.

However, the above findings have one serious implication. If there was any effective quality control system in place, then presumably serious cases would receive more careful screening and diagnosis would be made earlier in the process. Likewise there would tend to be fewer breaches of established procedure in serious cases because quality control measures would be directed at insuring that in these cases established procedures were followed. The pattern of findings so far observed does not suggest that any well directed system of quality control either formal or informal is operating.

Are Specific Evidence Gathering Activities Associated with Particular Kinds of Quality Control Failure or Case Outcome?

Police identifications

Out of a total of 14 cases in which police identification was an issue, 11 cases also involved errors in information processing. This proportion is larger than would be expected by chance.

Detectives carry a store of descriptions in their heads based on their own experience and criminal intelligence. This store of information is often applied under less than ideal conditions – someone who is acting suspiciously in the street may be "recognised". A decision to arrest on suspicion may be made. The circumstances and the recognition feeling reinforce one another and make it more difficult for the officer to accept or seek contrary evidence. The sample yielded clear examples of this phenomenon at work.

Alternatively individual cases can reach a state of complexity in which descriptive details are transposed in officers' minds resulting in mistaken identifications. While HOLMES procedures help to guard against such errors the sample contains examples of complex cases where such procedures were either not used or did not identify information processing errors leading to false positive identifications.

Police statements

In the 23 cases where police statements were problematic there was a greater than expected chance that communication errors had arisen especially between the CID and other agencies (the Crown Prosecution Service and the courts). This association is statistically significant. (x^2=9.48, df=1, p=.002)

In practice errors in police statements tend to promote ambiguity and uncertainty. When case files containing such statements are passed along the system, confusion arises. In a number of cases in the sample this confusion either gave the impression that the police officer's evidence was unreliable or that subsequent evidence, given in an attempt to clear up initial confusion, was fabricated. It is no surprise therefore that there is a clear association between problems with police statements and aspersions being cast in court on the probity of the police. This association is also statistically significant. (x^2=11.8, df=1, p=.0006)

Independent witness statements

There is a tendency for information processing errors to occur in cases where independent witness statements are implicated in the quality control failure. This tendency only approaches statistical significance but nevertheless seems worth comment because of the nature of the cases which give rise to the relationship. A typical example of how this association occurs would be as follows:

> an independent witness provides a statement which, because it appears to fit with what the investigating officer has already learnt about the case, he accepts. In fact the independent witness is saying something which does not support the case and at court this difference becomes apparent.

In CID mythology this is usually dismissed as witnesses not coming up to proof. The evidence in this study would suggest that saying that a witness has not come up to proof is a standard excuse but one which investigating officers themselves only use to others. In no case in which this kind of thing happened did the reporting officer resort to using this excuse to us although it would have been plausible for them to have done so.

In general strong independent witnesses make good cases against suspects. However, they can also induce a false sense of security, a sense that the case is closed. It is this risky idea that a case is closed or closing that can cause inconvenient bits of information to be left out of consideration or reinterpreted.

Admission statements
As might have been predicted, cases in which admission statements lie at the centre of the quality control issue are far more likely than other cases to involve errors with the PACE Act (13 out of 15 cases) and breaches of PACE rules (9 out of 15). Also all cases in which procedures for dealing with vulnerable suspects are not followed or rules are broken involve admission statements. (N=6)

PACE procedures and rules are especially vulnerable to interviews which take place off the record. During such interviews what is to be said on the record is decided. These informal interviews allow freer use of the techniques formerly commonplace in CID interviews in general (see Irving 1980).

Deliberate breaches of rules and procedures are obviously recognised as such by investigators particularly if the breaches are negotiated with suspects. Successfully negotiated breaches of the rules give officers protection from exposure as long as the agreement holds and nothing happens later in the investigation to make exposure inevitable. The evidence from our interviews and case records however is that decisions to break the rules frequently involve ignoring possible negative consequences and/or miscalculating the probability of their occurrence. We are not concerned here with the impropriety of such decisions, only with the quality of the decision-making involved. To this end we treat all decisions to break the rules as decisional errors. This raises the question of whether officers reported these cases to us on the basis of hindsight or to explain their own wrong-doing post hoc. Neither possibility sits comfortably with the evidence. Officers appeared genuinely worried by their failure to assess their vulnerability correctly and there was genuine irritation at the way their breaches of the rules had reduced the probability of obtaining a conviction in the given case. Moreover the hindsight might just as easily have been foresight if the decisions had been more carefully taken or supervised. While this implies considerable scope for improved training and supervision, there are individual differences in attitudes to rule-keeping and the impact of these differences are dealt with in the review of the interview findings.

In tune with the deliberate nature of these breaches of the PACE Act proportionately more cases involving admission statements were identified as quality control failures by the police themselves compared with other cases (in which diagnosis was more common at court or in the pre-trial period).

A third of the admission statement cases brought to us had not yet been tried. In these cases the officers concerned were expressing anxiety as to whether what had happened would come out in court or not. They tended to be sanguine about the outcome either because there was, they believed, no way for the defence to establish what had happened or because the procedural breach had been negotiated with the suspect, and the defence were therefore not expected to have an interest in the issue.

Is There a Relationship Between Domain of Error and Cause?

We need to establish whether any one error domain has more than its expected share of the three broad categories of error 'cause' we are working with (ie. reasoning errors deduced from a failure to foresee consequences; information processing errors and communication errors). The following was observed:

- Information processing as an error cause does not make itself felt in any particular "domain"

- In four cases out of the five in which forensic evidence was contaminated by the investigators, this occurred as a result of police officers failing to foresee the consequences of their actions

- Communication failures do not predominate in any one domain

Our three human factor error causes (reasoning, information processing and communication) are thus spread fairly evenly through the various domains of error we have described. A larger sample might however start to demonstrate biases.

ALTERNATIVE CLASSIFICATIONS OF ERROR

We have now examined the way types of evidence, domains of error and causes of error interact. In the theoretical introduction we described how the nature of a task can affect the kinds of error made in pursuit of that task. We went on to argue that any task performance demands the exercise of certain cognitive skills and errors could also be classified by skill across tasks.

Finally we suggested that certain factors in police work had already been identified as stressors and that these factors would tend to predict where errors would occur.

The scope of this study does not allow any proper testing of these classificatory principles but even with this small number of detailed case histories a start can be made in examining what kinds of prominent examples fall into the main categories of each of the classifications. This is akin to the kind of classifying activity which any explorer in new territory will engage in. Working with preexisting classifications, the most prominent features of flora and fauna for example, will be fitted to appropriate categories where that is possible. The classifier looks for items which either defy classification or for classes which are redundant or inappropriate. Where preexisting classifications are well established it is unlikely that they will be radically questioned except by very extensive sampling. However new examples will reinforce the classifications' usefulness and lend coherence to sets of otherwise chaotic data. This is the situation in this study.

Not surprisingly, we have found it very easy to classify the most prominent features of the case histories according to these three sets of principles. However it has been difficult to find a persuasive means of presenting the results. We have decided to limit the degree of detail we report to protect the anonymity of our informants. But even if this had not been so, we believe that it is preferable to extract precise examples from the case histories and present them in simple generic terms. To this end the essential features of each case were extracted and summarised as each case was analysed. The following listing of examples in each category is the shortest list which could be found which best expressed the variation in the sample of case histories.

It will quickly become apparent that there is a considerable level of overlap between these classifications. However, they have very different potential uses and we have therefore reported all three.

The "task" classification should ultimately help supervisors design and execute their supervisory function. The cognitive skill classification is more relevant to training: trainers need to be aware of what kind of skills they are seeking to improve. Lastly, the stress factor classification is most appropriate to the manager concerned with increasing quality control by exercising strategy options.

More extensive research will undoubtedly refine these classifications and produce comprehensive lists of examples within classes. Our aim here is to introduce the conceptual schema with enough examples to indicate their usefulness.

I. A classification of error based on task

The primary investigative tasks forming the basis of this classification are as described in the theoretical introduction.

A. *Find a Lead and Recognise it for What it is*

Performance of this investigative task has been marred by the following errors manifest in at least one case history:

- an intrinsically unreliable witness identification is accepted without proper validation

- false positive police identification is made leading to unlawful arrest

- assumptions of guilt are wrongly inferred from the MO in a linked crime

- evidence identifying a suspect is accepted when there were grounds for inferring that it might be malicious

- the word of the loser that a crime had been committed is accepted uncritically when technically it had not

- identification of a prime suspect from an informant who is falsely attributed with expert status is accepted uncritically

- the probity and reliability of an informant is accepted uncritically

B. *Avoiding Missing Relevant Information*

The following observed errors are relevant:

- police identification statements failed to describe the conditions of observation

- failures to establish continuity in the chain of evidence (usually linking stolen property to suspect)

- the language of police statements was ambiguous

- essential witness statements were not obtained

- control samples for forensic tests were not obtained

- essential documentation in a fraud case was not obtained

- essential real evidence was not secured

- tests of identification were not obtained

- corroboration of an admission was not sought

C. Extract Valid and Reliable Information from Suspects and Witnesses and Draw Valid Conclusions

The following issues arose in the case histories:

- eye-witnesses were assessed as reliable but failed to testify

- breaches of PACE rules invalidated admissions

- vulnerable suspects were not correctly managed according to PACE rules

- an interviewing officer was not properly briefed by the investigating officer, producing an inadequate interview result

- police statements prepared under pressure produced unreliable evidence

- unreliable expert testimony was not revealed by appropriate checking

- contamination of forensic evidence was allowed to occur

- false corroboration was accepted without checking

D. Communicate Accurately with Colleagues and Others about the Above

Examples are:

- no proper debrief was mounted following a team operation resulting in conflicting evidence which did not come to light until court

- letters to and from the CPS and court process offices went astray, resulting in evidence not reaching the right court at the right time and the case being wrongly scheduled

- documents and notices of various kinds although requested were not supplied

- CPS were not told background details of cases in particular when Regional Crime Squad informants were involved, leading to sudden damaging revelations in court

- notices of alibi arrived too late for investigation

- requests to witnesses to attend court did not arrive or were materially inaccurate

- officers were absent and failed to receive or send vital information because they were on other business or leave

E. Envisage what Level of Proof would be Sufficient and Use Available Information to Construct a Case

Problems which arose on this topic were as follows:

- failure to back-up evidence the reliability of which was likely to be attacked by the defence

- failing to foresee defence tactics which would invalidate the proof offered

- risky bending of rules and breaching of procedures likely to invalidate case if disclosed in court

- over-reliance on crude unvalidated evidence of identification

- attempts to appease the Regional Crime Squad (RCS) concerns about identifying informants putting proof at risk

- failure to foresee that the pattern of relationships between statements might create the impression of collusion and conspiracy

- difficulty of explaining post discovery, why errors should not be taken to indicate police malpractice

F. Maintain Accurate Recording

Examples of error were as follows:

- estimates of distance wrongly recorded

- dates and times confused

- places, people and incidents transposed

- addresses wrongly recorded

- letters wrongly addressed

- forensic samples wrongly labelled

II. A classification of error based on cognitive skill

A. *Memory:*

- a black face was misremembered leading to a false arrest

- police witnesses reported going beyond their memories in constructing statements after what they felt to be a frustrating public order incident

- memory errors were made in constructing statements late at night while those involved were emotionally overwrought

- in a complex case involving many suspects the size of the management task produced various lapses of memory as officers sought to control the volume of information

- under pressure in court a police witness forgot a vital rule of evidence

- police eye-witness' memory became confused under cross examination by the unexpected presentation of conflicting evidence

B. *Perceptual Discrimination and Acuity*

Examples:

- false positive identifications

- recording errors in custody records

- identifying marks missed on a weapon

- difficulties with visual discrimination during public order incidents in which officers came into violent contact with many individuals who later had to be identified

NB: While it may be that perceptual problems lurk behind a number of quality control issues, they are rarely consciously experienced. Our data are therefore not a very useful source of information on this issue.

C. *Vigilance and Attention*

Examples:

- relationship with informants not watched carefully enough

- failure to check that important communications arrive

- failure to spot that a variety of recording and procedural errors had been made

- failure to attend to a variety of details of case preparation which ultimately adversely affected the case in court

NB Vigilance and attention are components of most information processing errors. Once an error has been made it can only be corrected by appropriate levels of vigilance. All errors which persist in a work system are therefore ultimately examples of failure to apply due levels of vigilance and attention.

D. *Reasoning*
Examples:

- short-comings in a chain of evidence not identified

- crucial defence strategy not foreseen

- consequences of breaches of PACE rules not worked out

- probabilities of error associated with identifications not assessed correctly

- failure to correctly identify how investigative actions will appear when presented in court

- failure to hold onto alternative hypotheses in building case against a prime suspect

E. *Decision Making*
Examples:

- costs of breaching rules etc not taken into account

- probabilities of a negative outcome associated with procedural short-cuts wrongly estimated

- alternative plans of action in an investigation not assessed before a choice is made

- incompatible decisions taken with respect to disclosure of information to CPS at two points in the investigative process

- decisions made by default: ie. no action taken until too late to choose

- decisions about evidence made on police oriented cost benefit analysis which turns out to be invalid for CPS/trial

F. Communication
Examples:

- CPS not provided with essential information

- CPS fail to give police notice of need for witnesses to appear

- cases scheduled in ways which make it impossible for police witnesses to operate effectively

- messages sent but not received

- inappropriate channels of communications chosen

- levels of redundancy in communications too low resulting in failure

- no feedback on communication sent out

- discontinuity in a network: A communicates with B and C who do not communicate with each other in spite of their need to do so (frequently A is the Crown Prosecution Service and B and C are police officers)

- conflicting communications in a network often involving the Regional Crime Squad, the CID and the Crown Prosecution Service

- failure to share pertinent information re criminal intelligence among colleagues

III. A classification of error based on stressors

A. Equipment Failures
- problems with an admission statement exacerbated by tape failure

- difficulties with the use of video equipment and managing video evidence

B. Shiftwork
- rapid/frequent changes in work routine named as cause of failure to notify colleagues of absence

- over long periods of duty led to loss of attention and impairment of cognitive functioning in report writing

- decision to hold an irregular interview with a suspect made apparently as a result of having to go off duty before formal interview was possible

- shift/roster system fails to supply adequate manpower to meet demand created by a major operation – the result was paperwork not prepared adequately

C. Overload
- a case mushroomed creating serious work management problems

- unexpected public order problem stretched available resources beyond reasonable limits with consequent effect on handling suspects, obtaining evidence etc.

D. Courts
- inexperienced/under-briefed officers made errors under cross examination

- officers performed badly when their integrity was impugned by defence and they had no time/resources to offer rebuttal

- status of judge and trial procedure precluded arguing against unfair procedural decisions which placed police at an unreasonable disadvantage (in their eyes)

- officers afraid to make a clean breast of errors in court because of attitudes of lawyers

E. Emotional Involvement
- protective feeling for an identification witness leads officer to choose to make a procedural error

- a police witness in a case involving an assault on a colleague makes a simple evidentiary error

- friendliness with suspect led to breaking PACE rules

- over protective relationship with informants led to miscommunication with CPS

- authoritarian attitudes led to misattribution of expert status to certain high status role holders claiming authority they did not have

- personal anger at crime led to charging on insufficient evidence

F. Role Conflicts Within and Between Organisations

- CID officer and uniformed colleague clashed on attitudes to irregular interviewing and produced conflicting accounts

- custody officer made a humanitarian decision which allowed important evidence to be lost

- a vital ID parade was not held to spare the witness unpleasantness, leading to an effective challenge in court

- statements were edited to protect RCS informers at their request

- a trial was scheduled by the CPS in such a way that an investigating officer's preparatory work was rendered useless and the case was inadequately presented in court

- a judge accepted an alibi without enquiring of the investigating officer if its late notification had allowed it to be investigated

- a defence was shown to be false in court only after the officer in the case took advantage of an unexpected recess to test and expose what would otherwise have been accepted as fact: the court rules clashed with CID requirements

G. Career Development and the Organisational Culture

- poor performance in court was blamed on insufficient training, practice and supervision

- shortcomings in outcome from interviews blamed on poor interview training

- excessive workload on junior officers explained in terms of ambitions of supervising officer

- breaches of PACE seen in terms of pressure to get results and maintain promotion prospects even in the face of possibility of disciplinary action

- failure to admit errors in court explained in terms of judge's ability to spoil career prospects either directly or indirectly via complaint to senior officers

- colluding to hide errors seen as dictated by need to keep the system running efficiently and protect interests of those in authority

Commentary

In general informants provided us with detailed information about the work that was being done when errors were made. They also provided adequate descriptions of strings of events leading to errors and prevailing conditions when errors were made. These data were complemented by what could be extracted from the official version of events held on file. Individual motivation and many of the feelings engendered by the critical factors in each case history were also fairly accurately reported. However, people are not used to reporting on the way in which they exercise various skills and this shows in the kind of examples we have been able to adduce for the cognitive skill classification. Before this classification can be useful to trainers, additional research will be needed.

If the reader is tempted to see some of the examples as blindingly obvious (ie. predictable) then remember that this is the crux of our argument. Many of these errors are predictable; it is therefore remarkable that no training or supervision seems to be in place to avoid them.

This section of the report is intended to give police supervisors, trainers and managers a feeling for how human factors analysis relates to their jobs. It is not intended to add substantially to the body of findings. However classifying data in a number of apposite ways does emphasize particular phenomena because they find their way into the classifications at a variety of points. In most cases these phenomena have already been dealt with under other headings but two issues remain which need special mention.

First, there are numerous examples of failure to perform up to a standard which is required at some stage in the criminal justice process but is not necessarily required at the point at which action is taken. So, for example, a statement completed to a reasonable standard in the hours immediately after a long and arduous shift may look acceptable at the time but may turn out to be insufficient for its purposes at a later meeting with prosecution lawyers.

An act of casual kindness which, strictly speaking, breaches the PACE Act procedural rules, seems innocent enough until it is re-presented in court by the defence. In some cases seeing the theoretical consequences of potential courses of action and making operational decisions accordingly may require a level of inferential reasoning which officers do not possess but an equally powerful hypothesis is that officers may prefer to think in terms of managing discrete tasks, "clearing their desks", coping with the moment. They do not choose to see the immediate task in its wider criminal justice context. If this is the case, creating a system concept for investigating officers must be a priority training task. In any event it would be foolhardy to leave this hypothesis untested.

The second issue emerged directly from considering the courts as a special stressor. Classifying prominent elements of the case failures under this heading revealed that, regardless of the exact nature of an error, its exposure in court was often seen as personally distressing. This was particularly the case if defence lawyers impugned the probity of the police in relation to the error. This finding is confirmed statistically in the chapter reviewing the personal interview data.

Judges clearly have the power, whether they recognise it or consciously use it or not, to act as an informal disciplinary system. Investigators are concerned that judges' criticisms of them will affect their promotion prospects even though a trial is obviously not the place to assess or interpret an officer's performance. In extreme cases we understand that a judge can make a formal complaint to a Chief Constable but this is very rare; what seems to be more common is admonishment from the bench, and the use of the judge's discretion to stop a case or direct an acquittal informally to sanction the police. This imputation of a disciplinary motive to the judge cannot be substantiated in those few cases where it was alleged in this sample, but these interpretations of the behaviour of the Bench are a clear link between the court and personal stress. A second leg of this same issue is the way in which career and promotion prospects play a part in quality control failures. Errors can be forced on subordinate officers by career-motivated pressure from above or by individual officers trying too hard to please superiors for the same reason. But if overall quality of performance was the overriding consideration in appraisal then this career generated conflict would be less likely to arise. In fact it is not currently feasible for junior officers to resist, for example, time pressure from above on the ground of quality assurance. And the junior officer seeking promotion still has to show his worth on relatively crude indicators which may well conflict with measures of total quality performance.

PERSONAL CHARACTERISTICS OF THE SAMPLE OF OFFICERS WHO REPORTED CASES

Having put out a general request for information to CID officers and taken 60 case histories, we wished to know something about those police officers who had chosen to help us.

By obtaining background information for each police informant it also became possible to test whether certain kinds of officers reported certain types of error. In an exploratory study of this kind such information cannot of itself be used to test hypotheses, but it is a useful means of generating them. It should be kept in mind that as the sample did not cover officers who did not report errors to us, we cannot generalise our findings.

To obtain background information about the officers in the sample and some relevant attitudinal data, a telephone survey was conducted of the police officers reporting cases. In all 51 officers were contacted and interviewed. No-one contacted refused to take part but nine officers could not be contacted within the timetable of the study.

Method

The original data were fairly fine-grained: officers reported their actual age, years of experience and attitudes were recorded on semantic scales of various lengths. However with such a small sample this detailed data had to be recoded into either two or three categories per variable to facilitate statistical analysis. Results reported below use the final broad categories but we have included in appendix A a report of the original data and associated frequency counts.

Rank and Experience

The majority of the officers were either Detective Constables or Detective Sergeants (86%).

The sample distributions for age, length of police service and length of CID service were as follows:

Figure 1: Age distribution of officers

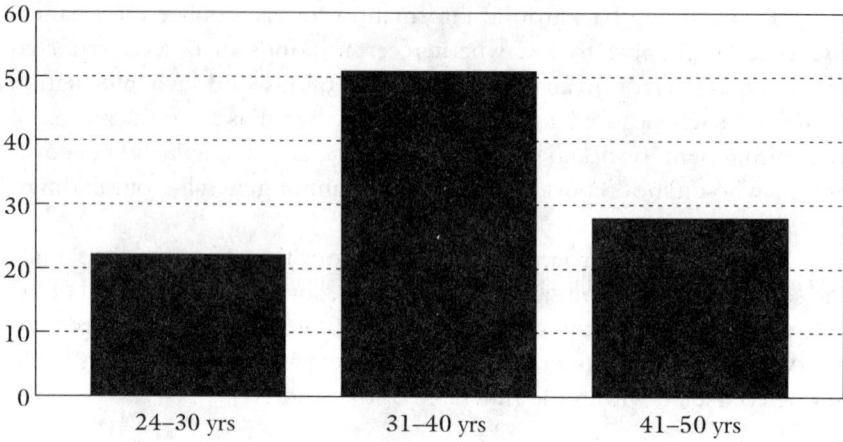

Age
Percent in each category

Figure 2: Years of service of officers

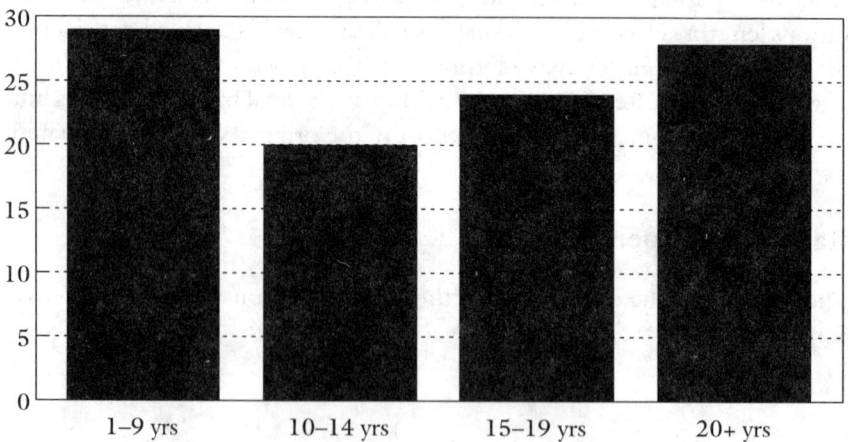

Years of Service
% in each class

Figure 3: CID experience of officers

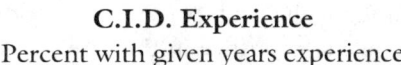

C.I.D. Experience
Percent with given years experience

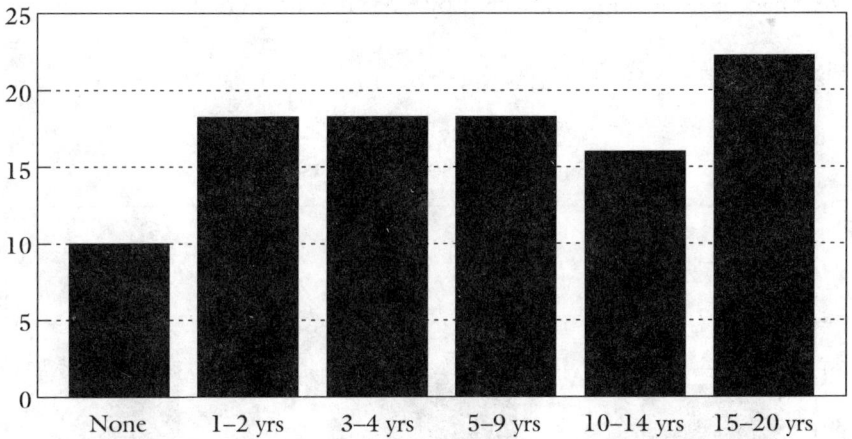

There is clearly no suggestion in these findings that quality control problems exemplified by the case histories are simply the product of lack of experience. However, as we shall see, there are some kinds of mistakes and errors which are associated with age and level of experience.

Reasoning

We wished, without being intrusive, to get some idea of the formal reasoning ability of individuals in the sample because errors of reasoning and failure to work out the consequences of actions were crucially involved in some of the case histories. We therefore asked for details of maths and science "O" and "A" levels as a crude indicator. Half the sample had a maths or science "O" level and 16% had a maths or science "A" level. Reasoning errors were as likely in the more as in the less qualified group.

Court experience

Experience of court work is relevant to knowing what can go wrong with cases and therefore being able to take effective evasive action. A third of the sample said they were very experienced at both magistrates and crown court work; 12% admitted to being inexperienced in crown court and 20% in magistrates court. It is indeed the case that lack of experience in court is related to making certain types of error and details of relevant correlations are reported below.

Reactions to errors

37% of the sample thought the problem they had reported had had a very severe effect on the quality of justice in the case concerned but very few (8%) had been personally affected by what had happened.

Figure 4: Gravity of effect

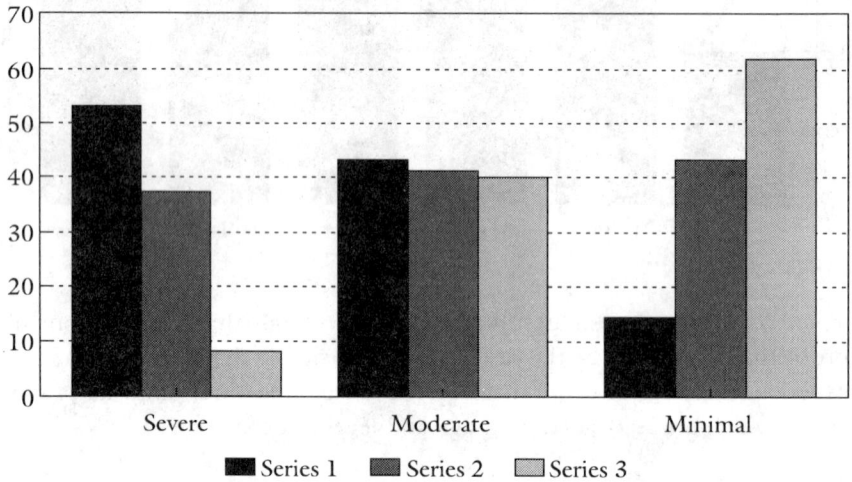

Series 1 = Overall effect,
Series 2 = Person effect,
Series 3 = Effect on criminal justice.

Emotional reactions to being involved in the quality control problem as reported were in the main anger and irritation (53%) and disgust and despair (20%). 16% said they were apathetic and 10% said they were surprised or amused.

Attitude to rules

As some cases had gone awry because of breaches of rules and procedures relating to the PACE act, we asked officers to rate themselves as rule keepers (high, medium or low) both generally and under pressure to obtain results.

Half the sample (51%) said they were high rule keepers; 18% admitted to being low. Under pressure the 51% went down to 33% with the increase being in the median category of the 3 point scale. Those who admitted being low rule keepers were exclusively older, very experienced CID officers.

Quality Control

70% of the sample felt their case could have been saved by better quality control but there was disagreement about how best to achieve it. 35% opted for better training, 20% for better supervision, 28% for better procedures and 18% for better communication.

Blame

Finally, we asked officers who they blamed for the errors that they had reported. The results were as follows:

Figure 5: Who gets the blame?

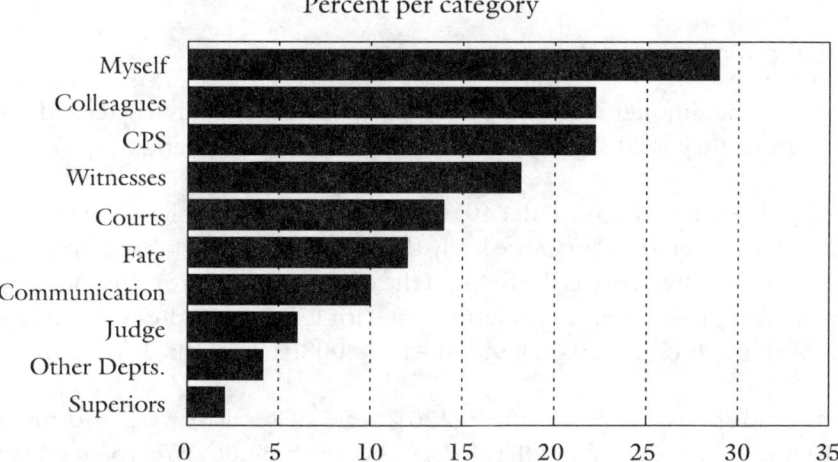

Who gets the blame
Percent per category

Bivariate analysis

The personal data about our informants allowed us to look for clues about the aetiology of the observed quality control problems in correlations between personal data and case characteristics. The kind of questions for which we ultimately need answers in this field are:

- which types of error are related to experience/age?

- is formal reasoning ability a factor in quality control?

- do certain kinds of error produce a strong emotional response in those involved?

- is blame apportioned differently for different kinds of error?

- are solutions seen in general terms or do they relate to recent experience of quality control issues?

- do personal ethics make a difference?

It would be naive to expect more than clues out of a sample of 60 cases and 51 personal interviews; however as we shall see, the clues which do emerge are highly plausible and worth pursuing on that basis alone given the significance to the criminal justice system of cutting down investigative error.

The level of statistical association between variables has been tested using a standard Chi-square test with appropriate corrections for small cell size. Where necessary, to conform with the rules on cell-size for the Chi-square test, categories have been collapsed.

Effects of age and experience

In general although age and police experience are highly correlated, as variables, they yield slightly different and revealing correlations.

Younger officers (under 40) reported all the cases which we classed as trivial. the over 40s were more likely than the rest to report cases involving confession statements as the focus of the quality control problem and were more likely to have either made an error with PACE procedures or actually broken the PACE rules. (x^2=9.7, df=1, p=.008; x^2=7.7, df=1, p=.02).

More experienced officers (20+ years of service) were also more likely to have breached PACE rules (x^2=3.6, df=1, p=.06). We would expect those with long established CID working practices to find adaptation to the PACE Act most difficult.

However there is a countervailing tendency for experienced officers to be less likely to report cases involving particular investigative errors. In particular, more experienced officers did not tend to report cases involving problems of continuity of evidence (x^2=3, df=1, p=.08) and they were also less likely to report that the absence of a colleague was a causal factor in their cases (x^2=5.6, df=1, p=.02).

Finally those with particular experience of crown court proceedings were less likely than others to be tripped up by unforeseen circumstances as cases developed (x^2=12.8, df=1, p=.0004).

This latter finding which is highly significant statistically raises questions about the locus of supervision. If in the future officers are going to have less experience of court as the result of the introduction of the Crown Prosecution Service and court experience helps avoid certain kinds of errors then either the CPS will need to take responsibility for eliminating those errors or the deficit in experience will need to be made up by training.

Effective reasoning ability

Mathematical ability as evinced by maths or science qualifications is a crude indicator of the capacity for logical reasoning. Given the laws of evidence and the burden of proof in criminal cases, the construction of a satisfactory case would seem to require a fair degree of logical ability. If errors are more likely among those without certain significant educational qualifications, this may indicate the need to impose some kind of selection test on CID candidates.

In fact none of the characteristics of the cases reported relate to the measure of reasoning ability that we have used. While this may well mean that the measure itself is invalid, it should be noted that errors in continuity of evidence and errors caused by failing to foresee how cases will develop (both requiring reasoning ability) are less likely among more experienced detectives. In this sample, and we suspect more generally in the police service, there is no correlation between experience and the indicator of reasoning ability. While our evidence is very thin, it is nevertheless worth proposing the hypothesis that experience of how the courts work and how cases go through the system is more valuable to detectives than formal logical reasoning ability within broad limits. Again, if proved, this would have implications for the choice of CID supervisors – wisdom may perhaps be preferable to "cleverness".

The above analysis, on the basis of sparse negative evidence, is presented mainly to indicate the utility of the general approach adopted in this study. It is not intended that it should be relied upon without further research.

Emotional responses

We have seen that, in general, officers see the problems contained in these cases as having an effect on the criminal justice system rather than on them personally.

However, it is also the case that certain types of error do have an impact on individual officers in an emotional sense.

There is a significant association between an officer saying that the case severely affected him personally and the error in the case resulting in the probity of the police being impugned in court ($x^2=4.7$, df=1, p=.04). This does not support the view of investigating officers as hardened professionals impervious to the cut and thrust of the adversarial system.

Likewise in cases in which errors occurred in police identification of suspects, the officers involved tended to be affected personally ($x^2=8.4$, df=1, p=.004). We suspect, looking back at the stories of these cases, that identifying the wrong person or failing to validate one's suspicions correctly are particularly painful to police professional pride.

Who gets the blame?

The findings on emotional response to the reported errors suggested that while the response itself was quite strong, the effect was only felt personally under particular circumstances (q.v.).

In contrast, there is a quite marked tendency for officers reporting errors to blame first themselves, then those closest to them in an organisational sense and then those they have to collaborate with most closely outside the organisation to get the job done.

It would be too easy to treat these findings as predictable: they might just as easily have been the other way round. In fact, at an anecdotal level the "canteen culture" does put them round the other way.

These results are encouraging from the psychologist's point of view: they suggest a reasonably high level of motivation to change if an appropriate lead and training are made available. We can shed a little more light on this issue by looking at correlations between attribution of blame and types of error.

Blaming Self

Those who break the PACE rules are more likely to take responsibility for it themselves than the sample as a whole ($x^2=3.2$, df=1, p=.07). While this result only approaches significance it is too important (as opposed to significant) to overlook. If breaches of PACE rules tended to be seen as the result of other pressures or faults in the system then designing action to improve quality in this area would be more complicated.

The only other correlation with blaming self is a negative tendency: those who reported that errors were due to unforeseen circumstances did not blame themselves ($x^2=5.4$, df=1, p=.02). On the surface, this is an unremarkable finding – why should they! But in all the cases upon which this negative correlation is based the unforeseen circumstances were eminently foreseeable. In contrast to the PACE rule breakers therefore, this constitutes a more complex quality control issue. If officers fail properly to foresee risks or weaknesses in their cases and then exonerate themselves from the ensuing difficulties, it is far more difficult either to persuade them they need training, or to impose external controls.

It is in these circumstances that peer group review can be a useful tool: officers who suffer from an inability to work out the consequences of their own or others' action can, with this technique, come to an understanding of their difficulty. Imposing blame from above in such cases merely reinforces the tendency towards self exoneration. Supervisors should review cases which have come unstuck apparently because of things beyond investigating officers' control with this finding in mind. A too easy acceptance by management of the malign influence of chance or fate can actually make review procedures counter-productive.

Blaming Colleagues

Crime investigation is a team effort in most non-trivial cases. It is therefore not surprising that most correlations between blame variables and types of error occur in this category. The relevant variables and their significance levels are listed below:

Table 7
Correlation between blaming colleagues and types of error

Variables description	x^2	df	significance
Error in a police statement	10.68	1	.001
Error in a police identification	10.52	1	.001
Perceptual or other information processing error	6.61	1	.01
Errors resulting in doubt being cast on police probity	4.18	1	.04
Errors in establishing continuity of evidence	4.05	1	.04

Where an investigative error is seen as a team responsibility, then the supervising and quality control mechanism to combat it must be based on the team and not on the individual. When an officer makes an observation or records it, then at the time it may be sufficient for his purposes but later in the hands of another officer at another point in the investigative process it becomes insufficient. It is one of the prime responsibilities of management to provide clear guidelines on quality standards at all stages in a production process so that those at the beginning are not unfairly blamed for the failure of their work to live up to what is expected of it (unknown to them) later in the process.

It is worth noting that only 2 officers blame themselves *and* colleagues (the logical position in a team situation).

Blaming the CPS

Only one significant relationship emerges from the analysis: there is a slight tendency for the CPS to be implicated in instances where errors are the result of officers' absence from their posts (x^2=4.5, df=1, p=.03). In view of other findings on communication between departments and agencies it would seem sensible to check communication back-up for those on leave or absent on courses. Do mail redirection mechanisms exist? Are phone calls redirected? What happens to fax and other e-mail traffic?

Blaming Witnesses

As witnesses, the victims of assault can create severe problems for investigating officers. Never more so than in cases of domestic violence. Assault victims can change their minds about their complaint; seek to invalidate their own evidence; contradict themselves or become defendants in cases brought by their assailants. Problems with victim statements are associated with blaming witnesses (x^2=5.8, df=2, p=.02). Given what is now known about domestic violence victims and the procedures that have been evolved to deal with their complaints, there may be room for widening the application of such procedures or adapting them for equally fraught areas such as public brawls, vendettas and the like.

Blaming Other Departments

The two cases of errors made with real evidence both involved Scenes of Crime and forensic laboratory errors.

Quality control

The sample was almost equally divided between the four main ways of attacking the quality control issue: there are no statistically significant relationships between preferred ideas about improving quality control and aspects of reported cases. It may be that officers have a variety of human error experience and it is the sum total of experience which sets their minds on a preferred solution, it may be that, like methods of study, preferred methods of quality control are related to individual cognitive style. It is anyway the case that Total Quality Management, which is the current touchstone in this area, advocates a systemic approach in which all the possible sources of quality improvement are brought into play.

Personal ethics

We specifically asked officers to rate themselves as rule keepers because of the frequency with which PACE act rules and procedures and indeed general force procedures were disregarded in the sample of case histories. It is therefore startling to find that those who labelled themselves as low rule keepers were not more likely than others to have been involved in reported cases where breaches of PACE act procedures were at issue.

However, of the nine cases in the sample which were withdrawn by the prosecution because of the errors involved, eight were reported to us by officers who rated themselves as low rule keepers. It may be that PACE act rules are currently too high profile for experienced officers (as low rule keepers are: q.v.) to chance their arms.

Low rule keepers were significantly more likely than others to be involved in cases where communication problems had been caused by the absence of someone ($x^2=5.6$, df=1, p=.02).

This suggests a rather more trivial kind of rule bending to do with time keeping and personal discipline. We believe this unexpected pattern of findings needs further detailed investigation. For example it would be important to know whether personal discipline over such things as presence or absence, helps or hinders the development of concern for higher order ethics.

CONCLUSIONS AND RECOMMENDATIONS

Summary of Main Findings

1. Errors of the kind described in this report are not normally recorded on files. Feedback from court cases or other external sources is often known to those involved in the case but is not formally recorded for future quality control purposes.

2. Although standing orders and established procedures may suggest otherwise, there are no proactive and focused quality control procedures incorporated into the supervision of CID officers.

3. The supervisory function in CID's is craftlike in conception and protects the 'craft' autonomy of detectives.

4. The study suggests that the majority of CID operational errors are diagnosed by the courts, or by the CPS in the pre-trial period.

5. While CID officers are generally aware of the ways in which investigations can go wrong, they are almost wholly unaware of human factors phenomena in general and their own proneness to error in particular.

6. Training of detectives and their supervisors does not deal with human factors issues neither is it informed by any data on the kind of errors which are exemplified in this study. The reasons which lie

behind the various rules and procedures which officers are instructed to follow are not explained. Officers are not helped to foresee the consequences of breaking rules and subverting procedures. Reasoning skills and defences against cognitive error are not taught.

7. Cases reported by the Crown Prosecution Service do not differ qualitatively from those reported by the police.

8. The cases are fairly evenly split between crimes involving an element of violence and those which do not. However officers reported more serious than trivial cases to us.

9. Errors most frequently involved the following types of evidence: police statements (37% of cases), independent witness statements (30%), admission statements (25%), police identification statements (23%).

10. The most frequent "domains" of error found in the sample involved mistakes in the administration of the PACE Act (30%), breaches of PACE rules (22%) and problems with continuity of evidence (28%). In all half (53%) of the cases involved some kind of departure from established CID procedure.

11. Three general error "causes" were identified: failure to foresee and take account of circumstances which should have been foreseen (ie. errors of reasoning), errors in the processing of information and errors in communication. Each causal factor alone accounted for about a third of cases.

12. Of the 60 cases in the sample, 17% resulted in a guilty verdict; 46% were withdrawn, dismissed or found not guilty on direction; 20% were found not guilty. The rest were as yet undecided at the time the analysis was performed.

13. The evidence as presented to us tended to suggest that about half (17 out of 39) the lost cases would have resulted in convictions if errors had not been made. In only 4 cases did the errors made appear to increase the probability of a false conviction.

14. In 35% of cases the errors made led to charges of police impropriety in court. While legitimate as court tactics, these charges were generally exaggerated given contextual information about the error concerned which was available to us but not available in court.

15. The prominent elements of the case histories could be classified by task, skill and known stressor. However, evidence about skill deficits was poor because of the methodology.

16.   Classifying case elements by known stressors underlined the significance of the courts and career issues in quality control. In all three alternative classifications tried out in this analysis a ubiquitous issue was an apparent tendency among investigators to take a short-term rather than a wider system view in making risky decisions.

Human factor errors of predictable kinds occur in all the major components of CID work. These errors constitute quality control failures which, once they are diagnosed or revealed, investigating officers recognise as such.

While these quality control failures are recognised and were reported to us, it is not common practice to bring such failures to notice or record them unless that becomes inevitable because of disciplinary actions or the intervention of external agencies.

We can find no evidence in what has been reported to us that any formal or informal system of quality control aimed at minimising human factor error exists in the force and the review of training suggests that this is the case throughout the service. Moreover the cultural climate of the police service and the craft attitudes of CID officers would tend to militate against the development of the systems view of both CID work and the administration of criminal justice.

The quality control failures which occurred in the sample seem to result predominantly in the prosecution losing cases but given the nature of our sample and how we obtained it, this is scarcely surprising. However there is nothing about the errors observed which suggests that they could only occur in cases where the guilty were at risk of not being convicted.

We can say nothing about the overall incidence and prevalence of quality control failures. However the analysis of this small sample of cases makes a start at defining relative frequencies of different types of error. We can also confirm for these cases what is axiomatic in all accident research: that small errors can have serious consequences and vice versa. To an extent the numbers game is anyway a diversion: in criminal justice any human error which could cause a miscarriage needs to be taken seriously.

While conscious rule breaking is a factor to be reckoned with, it constitutes a small minority of all instances of quality control failure brought to us during the course of this study. Even in that small subsample of cases the investigators appeared to be motivated mostly by a desire to get the job done with minimum wasted effort. There is an obvious need to examine more ethically problematic cases by referring to discipline and complaints files so as to increase awareness of rule breaking which is both conscious and concealed or denied.

Recommendations

1. Improving the Availability of Data

Inappropriate and/or inadequate supervision and the police culture militate against investigating officers talking about human factors in quality control failures within the service. It is recommended that a confidential reporting system is set up along the lines available to airline pilots and nurses. The service, with linked capacity to analyse data and report on issues and trends could be located within the Police Federation or established entirely independently for example under the auspices of the Police Foundation or a suitable applied psychology or work research institute. Whether or not this recommendation is supported, further research is urgently required to test and refine the findings of this pilot project. The goal should be to break down cultural barriers to talking about and dealing constructively with human error in policing.

2. Training

It is recommended that work system and general ergonomic concepts be incorporated into appropriate training courses and that the notion of quality control systems for investigative work be introduced as soon as practicable into supervisors' and managers' courses. The aim should be to give all operational detectives and supervisors a working knowledge of the errors they are likely to make, the conditions likely to promote error and ways and means of minimising such errors.

3. Supervision

The subject of supervision is being addressed by other researchers reporting to the Royal Commission. We merely recommend our findings to them for consideration. We believe that the nature of supervisory practice and the relationship between supervisors and supervised will need to change if effective quality control measures are to be introduced – the measures *cannot* be introduced on the back of existing relationships and culture.

4. Inter-Agency Considerations

The courts and the Crown Prosecution Service must adapt to a reasonable view of how quality control failures in investigative work come about. There must be ways in which errors can more easily be brought to notice and corrected. Court procedure should not be used as a covert disciplinary sanction against the police. Urgent steps should be taken to try to minimise exaggerated inferences of malpractice arising from late diagnoses of errors taken out of context in court. To allow present trends to continue is likely to create a severe crisis of confidence if that point has not already been reached.

BIBLIOGRAPHY

Abercrombie, M L J (1960) *The Anatomy of Judgement:* Free Association Books, London.

Alexander, D A, Innes, G, Irving, B, Sinclair, S D and Walker, L D (1991) *Health, Stress and Policing*, Police Foundation, London.

Bailey, R W (1982) *Human Performance Engineering a Guide for System Designers*, Prentice-Hall, New Jersey.

Baldwin, J (1991) *Summarising Tape Recordings of Police Interviews*, Criminal Law Review, pp. 671–9.

Burrows, J (1986) *Burglary: police actions and victims' views*, Home Office Research and Planning Unit Paper 37, Home Office, London.

Cooper, C L and Marshall, J (1976) Occupational Sources of Stress: A review of the literature relating to coronary heart disease and mental ill health, *Journal of Occupational Psychology*, 49, 11–28.

Damodaran, L, Simpson, A and Wilson, P (1980) *Designing Systems for People*, NCC Publications, Manchester.

Davidson, M J and Veno, A (1977) *Multifaceted Aspects of Stress in the Police Service*, A C T Australian Institute of Criminology Press (Monograph, 187p.).

Davidson, M J and Veno, A in Cooper, C L and Marshall, J (Eds) 1980 *White Collar and Professional Stress.* John Wiley, London.

Deutsch, M (1973) *The Resolution of Conflict.* Yale University Press, New Haven.

Galer, I A R (1987) *Applied Ergonomics Handbook*, Butterworths, London.

HMSO (1991) The Human Element in Shipping Casualties, Marine Directorate, Department of Transport: HMSO, London.

Irving, B (1980) *Police interrogation. A Case Study of Current Practice*, Royal Commission on Criminal Procedure, Research Study No.2 HMSO, London.

Loftus, G R and Loftus, E F (1976) *Human Memory*, Lawrence Erlbaum, New Jersey.

Maguire, M, Noaks, L, Hobbs, R, Brearley, N (1992) *Assessing Investigative Performance*: unpublished MS.

Norusis, M J (1990) *SPSS/PC Base Manual*, SPSS Inc, Chicago Illinois.

RCCP (1980) *Royal Commission on Criminal Procedure*, Final Report. HMSO, London.

Rips, Lance T (1990) Reasoning Annu. Rev. Psychol. 1990: 41: pp 321–53.

Trist, E L, Higgin, G W, Murray, H and Pollock, A B (1963) *Organisational Choice*. Tavistock, London.

Welford, A T (1968) *Fundamentals of Skill*. Methuen, London.

Wickens, O (1984) *Engineering Psychology and Human Performance*, Merrill Columbus, Ohio.

Yerkes, R M and Dodson, J D (1908) The relation of strength of stimulus to rapidity of habit formation, *J Comp. Neurol. Psychol.*, 18, 459–482.

APPENDIX A

Interview schedule and frequency distributions

1.	What is your current rank?	N	%
	Detective Inspector/Inspector	3	6
	Detective Sergeant	15	29
	Detective Constable	29	60
	PC	4	8

2.	How many years of service have you completed overall?	N	%
	1–9 years	15	29
	10–14 years	10	20
	15–19 years	12	24
	20–30 years	14	28

3.	How many years service in the CID have you completed?	N	%
	0	5	10
	1–2 years	9	18
	3–4 years	9	18
	5–9 years	9	18
	10–14 years	8	16
	15–20 years	11	22

4.	How old will you be next birthday?	N	%
	24–30	11	22
	31–40	26	51
	41–50	14	28

5.	How many passes at "O" level did you obtain in Maths and Science?	N	%
	None	25	49
	One	13	26
	More than one	13	26

6.	How many at "A" level?	N	%
	One or more	8	16
	None	43	84

7.	How would you rate your experience of Crown Court work?	N	%
	Very experienced or experienced	17	33
	Fairly experienced	28	55
	Not experienced	6	12

8.	How would you rate your experience of Magistrates' Court work?	N	%
	Very experienced or experienced	17	33
	Fairly experienced	24	47
	Not experienced	10	20

9.	Taking all things into account how severe do you think the effect of the error in this case has been?	N	%
	Severe or very severe	26	53
	Fairly severe	16	33
	Not serious	7	14

10.	Thinking of its effect in criminal justice terms, how severe has it been?	N	%
	Severe or very severe	18	37
	Fairly severe	15	31
	Not serious	16	33

11.	Thinking of its effect on you personally, how severe has that been?	N	%
	Severe or very severe	4	8
	Fairly severe	7	14
	Not serious	31	62

12.	How would you describe your own emotional reaction to the case?	N	%
	Irritated/Angry	26	53
	Apathetic	8	16
	Disgusted/despairing	10	20
	Surprised/amused	5	10

13.	How would you rate yourself as a keeper of rules?	N	%
	High rule keeper	26	51
	Medium	16	31
	Low	9	18

14.	Now how would you rate yourself when under pressure to get results?	N	%
	High rule keeper	17	33
	Medium	25	49
	Low	9	18

15.	Thinking about your particular case, could the error have been avoided with quality control measures?	N	%
	Yes it could	35	70
	No it could not	15	30

16.	If you thought it could, how could that have been achieved?	N	%
	Training	14	35
	Supervision	8	20
	Procedures	11	28
	Communication	7	18

17.	Who do you blame for what happened?	N	%
	I blame:–		
	myself	15	29
	my colleagues	11	22
	superior officers	1	2
	other departments	2	4
	other forces	–	–
	the CPS	11	22
	the court system	7	14
	the judge/magistrate	3	6
	witnesses	9	18
	failures of interpersonal communication	5	10
	failures of inter-agency communication	5	10
	fate	6	12

A BRIEF REVIEW OF RELEVANT POLICE TRAINING

Barrie Irving and Ian McKenzie

Contents

A BRIEF REVIEW OF RELEVANT POLICE TRAINING

INTRODUCTION

Training which deals with the investigation of crime falls into five categories

- probationer training

- post probationer training for constables

- supervisory training (Sergeants, Inspectors and others): initial and developmental courses

- specialised training: detectives and interviewing skills etc.

- training for senior officers

Change in all these categories has been quite rapid over the past decade and that situation is continuing. A purely didactic style of teaching has given way to one which emphasises facilitation and uses the so called "fabric" approach through which the behavioural sciences have been introduced into police training via such innovative courses as the Metropolitan Police's "Human Awareness Training" for probationers. The "fabric" in this context is woven from new material drawn from the social sciences and more traditional content such as law and procedure. At the same time militaristic elements in training have been reduced or eliminated.

The new student-centred style of teaching is generally credited with creating a more effective learning environment (Cf Bruner, 1966, Fontana 1985).

Innovations in Metropolitan Police training have been followed closely by a similar major shake-up in national probationer training spearheaded by the Central Planning Unit (CPU) at Harrogate which is responsible for the design, development and evaluation of non-metropolitan police training courses and the training of trainers (see McDonald et al 1986).

Professor McDonald's report, which has been the catalyst for this expanded programme of innovation, had an impact on courses and methods well beyond his original remit to study probationer training.

Major changes have included softening the authoritarian and militaristic culture at training centres, adopting student centred methods and dropping formal written examinations where feasible, replacing them with skill assessment on the basis of role plays etc.

In general, major topics in training are now dealt with across a number of courses: subjects are no longer treated in discrete one-off blocks.

In reviewing the content of investigative training with special emphasis on avoiding miscarriages of justice we have therefore tried to develop a career-wide perspective on training provision in three salient areas.

- the management of suspects

- handling witnesses

- identification issues

SUSPECTS, WITNESSES and IDENTIFICATION

Suspects

The coercive treatment of suspects and the techniques of police interrogation have been a major source of concern both for lawyers and social scientists. The traditional approach of the police – to obtain a confession – has long been at loggerheads with Lord Devlin's (1979, p.71) assertion that, "confession is not the short cut to justice" for, as Mirfield (1985 p.9) put it, "Persuaded of the suspect's guilt by all the information available before interview and by his demeanour and verbal responses at interview, an officer's mind, it seems not unreasonable to suppose, may,..."reconstruct reality"."

Irving's (1980) study for the previous Royal Commission, demonstrated that the coercive elements of police interrogation practice (Irving, 1980; Hackett 1982; Irving and McKenzie, 1989) were commonplace. Although, following the introduction of the Police and Criminal Evidence Act 1984, Irving and McKenzie (1989) showed that the use of "tactics" had been substantially reduced, the "search for a cough" (confession) was not eliminated. However, case law generated since the Act, the comments of judges and a growing degree of public concern have had some effect. For example, Moston, Stephenson and Williamson (1990), the last a senior police officer, argued that there is a need to develop an information gathering, non-manipulative approach to interviews with suspects. These authors see the suspect-interview as an evidence gathering exercise; if the suspect does not confess, but can be shown to be lying, then that is, in itself, useful evidence which can be presented to a court. A confession, according to this view of interrogation, is not necessarily the goal of interviewing.

Those designated "at risk" by the Codes of Practice issued under the PACE Act constitute a crucial issue in the management of custodial interrogation and hence in relevant police training. Mentally ill and handicapped, deaf and dumb, blind and non-English speaking suspects pose both generic and idiosyncratic interviewing problems. This review

81

therefore examines both the extent to which coercive tactics remain the current coin of interview training and the issues connected with "at risk" persons.

Witnesses

As Bull *et al*, (1983 p.22) put it, "psychologists have known for decades that quite often people not only fail to see and hear everything presented to their senses, they also "see" and "hear" things which did not occur.

Evidence has accumulated which shows that witnesses can be unconsciously manipulated into producing inaccurate accounts of incidents as a consequence of the language used by the person gathering the information.

- Loftus and Palmer (1974) have shown that the "emotional" content of words selected to form a question (hit v. collided v. smashed) can cause considerable variation in witness estimation of speed (the more "violent" the verb the higher the estimated speed);

- that questions which imply, erroneously, that an object or event occurred, can lock that nonexistent event or object into a witness' memory;

- that "presuppositional questions" (phrased, "Did you see the...?") in contrast to simple probing questions (phrased, "Did you see a...?") produce a greater number of perceptions of non-present items, and that;

- questions containing emotional or powerful information can "prime" people's memory for events such that later, more (but related) distorted information is produced (more violent verbs used to elicit information about an accident also produced recollection of nonexistent broken glass).

This review will look at the extent to which this and other information about the problems associated with information gathering from witnesses, is incorporated into training.

Identification

As long ago as 1929 the Royal Commission on Police Powers and Procedures noted that when faced with a "line-up" of suspects on an identification parade, some witnesses, "may unconsciously tend to identify the person who most resembled their recollection of the culprit disregarding, apparently, the alternative that he may not be present at all." More recently, the Devlin Report (1976) noted that "recognition depends on the human ability to memorise a face, even when it cannot be described with any accuracy." In that assertion, the Devlin Committee recognised that there is a difference (established by psychologists) between the ability of a witness to identify a face they have seen before, and the more complex task of describing that face to others. Photofit pictures have been shown to be very insensitive instruments (Ellis and Davis 1977) which frequently lead to the construction of poor likenesses.

However, in experimental studies, Shepherd *et al* (1982) have shown that identification of persons in a line up is reasonably accurate, although severe decrements in the ability to select the "right" person occur after a year has elapsed. Estimations of accuracy based on variables existing in "real-life" situations are "uniformly low" (Bull *et al* 1983, p.31). More importantly, however, evidence exists (Deffenbacher, 1980) which suggests that witness confidence in the selection they have made either has no bearing on the true accuracy of their decision, or is negatively correlated with it. Put another way, the more confident people are about their decisions the less likely they are to be accurate.

In reviewing relevant training we will therefore examine the extent to which this and other information about the problems associated with facial identification by witnesses, are introduced.

METHODS AND SCOPE

Probationer and post probationer training

Members of the ACPO Training Committee have identified a number of points in the recruit/probationer training syllabi which are seen as "critical" in that they appear to address those elements of training, in both practice and procedure, at which potential miscarriages of justice could occur or be prevented. The identified points are as follows:

Police Probationer Training Foundation Course

Student Notes Module 1 –

F1/1 Appearing in court and giving evidence
F1/1 Pocket Book Rules

Police Probationer Training Foundation Course

Student Notes Modules 2,4 & 7 –

The Police Service – Statement of Common Purpose and Values

2/19/1 Effective Communication
2/20/1 Evidence
2/23/1 Identification Methods
2/32/1 Non-Verbal Communication
2/41/1 Questioning Suspects

Police Probationer Training (Second Year of Probation)

Post Foundation Student Notes –

PF/1 Dealing with detained persons
PF/1 Evidence

Post Probationer Training – Constables with two years+ service

Policing Skills Development Course –

Extracts from notes supplied to students:

Introduction to Communication
Barriers to Communication
Questioning
Listening Skills
Dealing with Witnesses
Dealing with Suspects
The Sub-Division Case Study

These items in the recruit syllabus have been examined at Chantmarle, Dorset (a Regional Training Centre, representative of the others located at

Ashford, Bruche, Cwmbran, Durham and Ryton-on-Dunsmore), as have similar items at the Metropolitan Police Training College at Hendon, London.

From the Central Planning Unit at Harrogate, copies of all "student notes" which relate to the above inputs were obtained and have been examined. Similar material has been obtained from the Metropolitan Police Training School at Hendon, and it too has been examined.

In addition, members of staff at the centres have been consulted and informally interviewed.

Uniform branch supervisory training

The Regional Training Centre at Middlemore (Exeter) which is run in premises of the Devon and Cornwall Police but draws students for sergeant and inspector courses from the South-West region, has been visited.

Copies of relevant "student notes" (produced for national use by the Central Planning Unit at Harrogate) were obtained and have been examined. Similar material has been obtained from the Metropolitan Police Training School at Hendon.

In addition, members of staff at the centres have been consulted and informally interviewed.

Specialised training (Detectives/Interviewing skills, etc.)

Visits were made to the Regional Detective Training School at Kings Weston, Bristol and to the Metropolitan Police Detective Training School at Hendon. In addition telephone contact was made with the Interview Development Unit of Merseyside Police and relevant topics were, as before, discussed with a number of senior officers and instructors.

Training for senior officers

Documentary evidence with regard to senior officer training was obtained and examined. An overview of the management of crime investigation (Dickenson, 1991) has been used as a basis for this part of the review. Senior officer training has been discussed with members of the ACPO Crime Committee.

PROBATIONER AND POST PROBATIONER TRAINING: COMMENTARY

Appearing in court and giving evidence

In both the Metropolitan Police Training School and the Regional Training Centres the factual input on "Appearing in court and giving evidence" is comprehensive. All training establishments address the need to present factual evidence on oath, to avoid opinion, give instruction about the use of notes (including the need for those notes to be made at the time or as soon as possible after the incident), to respond to cross-examination without argument, and to answer questions "frankly".

However, as was pointed out by an instructor at Hendon:

"The old Instruction Book [a police manual] used to say that evidence is supposed to be given impartially and that evidence for the accused is as important as that against him. We don't do that any more."

The Metropolitan Police Instruction Book (as amended at January 1970) carried the following words at Chapter 11 paragraph 13(1):

"When giving evidence, officers are required to state with accuracy all the facts known to them, un-influenced by the desire to injure or shield any one. THEY ARE UNDER AS CLEAR AN OBLIGATION TO INFORM THE COURT OF FACTS WHICH TELL IN FAVOUR OF THE ACCUSED AS OF FACTS WHICH TELL AGAINST HIM. This is an obligation which rests upon all witnesses but it rests in a special degree upon the police..." (emphasis in original.)

Given the thematic nature of current training and the discretion afforded to trainers this point may be handled informally but the change is worth noting.

Pocket Book Rules

Training establishments cover the rules about making notes in pocket books and elsewhere in a slightly different manner. They use a mnemonic "No E-L-B-O-W-S". For Regional Centres the letters signify:

	E	rasures
	L	ines missed out –
No	B	lank Spaces
	O	ver writing
	W	ritten in ink
	S	pare pages to be ruled through

whilst at Hendon the rules are:

No
E	rasures
L	leaves to be torn out
B	lank Spaces
O	ver writing
W	riting between the lines
S	tatements to be recorded in direct speech

While individual trainers may teach these rules differently and the concepts may be fleshed out over a number of courses, the following reservation expressed by a senior trainer at Hendon is significant:

> "We give them all these rules but I don't think we tell them why its necessary. They don't see it as a protection, either for themselves or for the suspect. It's just a chore."

Communication issues

The changes in recruit and probationer training have resulted in the introduction of the notion of "social skills of policing". In both training establishments, use is made of video both as a source of stimulus material and as a self-development tool. Drawing on the standard methods of social skills training used by psychologists and psychiatrists in clinical settings, officers are placed in numerous "role-play" situations in which they are faced with their peers or trainers playing the parts of members of the public who present them with "police problems" of varying complexity.

Responses to these stimuli are recorded on video (using hand held camcorders) and students are then subjected to immediate and comprehensive feedback on their performance. Criticism (both positive and negative) is given by trainers and by a student's peers. Tapes of performance are retained by the student for future use, and the whole tape is used as a record of the development of skill. In some, quite rare, cases the video record also serves as a source of evidence to justify a decision to dispense with the services of a recruit. The approach advocated by Shepherd (1984), Burns-Howell *et al*, (1981) and McKenzie (1983, 1984a, 1984b) is now commonplace.

This skills-based approach deals with effective communication, evidence, non-verbal communication and questioning suspects. In both training formats a Skills Evaluation Exercise (SEE) takes place over two days and consists of a number of "exercise stations". An exercise station may be a practical role play or a question paper exercise. Performance is evaluated by a member of staff who grades the student on the basis of predetermined criteria (See Appendix 1 and 2).

In general, the "thirty-nine steps to independent patrol" (see Appendix 3) are adequately addressed in the Foundation Course and in the Structured Work experience (CPU) or Street Duties Course (Met).

The Police and Criminal Evidence Act, 1984

In a general sense the content of the Police and Criminal Evidence Act 1984 is covered well in both training settings. The Codes of Practice and the relevant sections of the Act are on-going themes throughout the bulk of training. Indeed, there has been a major shift in emphasis in the last few years. In the past much training was defensive and concentrated on offering advice which sought to protect the officer from the misfortunes that might befall him or her if breaches of the rules or the legislation took place. There used to be a determination to demonstrate that the Police and Criminal Evidence Act did not work and could not be made to work. (McKenzie, Morgan and Reiner 1990). However the overwhelming contemporary concern amongst trainers is to encourage students to recognise the civil rights issues embedded in the Act and the Codes, and to encourage adherence because, "...it's proper behaviour and not because lawyers and politicians say so" (Instructor, Regional Training Centre.)

While this new direction is to be welcomed there are other aspects of the coverage which require attention.

"At Risk" suspects

In general training does not help the student to identify those who are "at risk". Juvenile suspects pose no difficulty: they can be readily identified. However, the role definition of "appropriate adult" makes finding one who will serve as such problematic in a wide range of cases. This topic is generally not addressed in training.

Similarly identifying the visually handicapped, and those whose speech and hearing is impaired is straightforward but in these cases finding appropriate support can require knowledge of what will be required and where to find it. These matters are not adequately dealt with in current training but this may well be because the required information is unavailable.

The Codes of Practice spell out the need for care with regard to the interviewing of suspects who are mentally handicapped or mentally ill. There is considerable evidence of the likelihood of suggestibility in suspects falling into these categories. Indeed, many of the most recent miscarriages of justice have involved mental vulnerability.

However as has been emphasised all too vividly by the Silcott appeal (R V Silcott etc. Times 9 December 1991), experts themselves cannot always agree on what constitutes "significant impairment of intelligence and social functioning". The codes of the Police and Criminal Evidence Act are intended to be fail safe ie. safeguards are meant to be applied if there is any risk that the suspect is vulnerable. But students still need to be instructed on the assessment of that risk.

The dilemma is summed up by one senior instructor at Hendon:

"To be quite truthful, even though I've been teaching this stuff since before PACE came out, I don't know the difference between mental handicap and mental illness."

Some instructors and senior officers at Chantmarle, at Middlemore, at Kings Weston and at Hendon, indicated that training in these areas is as good as it can be (ie., it emphasises "If there is the slightest suspicion..." etc.). They argue that it is foolish to expect officers to have sufficient skills and knowledge to be able to respond correctly when the experts cannot agree amongst themselves. While this view is understandable, in circumstances where more and more mentally handicapped people are surviving to adulthood and being cared for "in the community" more positive advice in training on this issue appears warranted.

Witnesses

The "communication" aspects of the Foundation Course and follow up probationer training provide adequate input with regard to the problem areas mentioned in the introduction. However, new psychological findings are not incorporated into training as they appear. There is an obvious difficulty in keeping material up-to-date.

Identification Methods

The requirements of legislation and the Codes of Practice are well covered but the emphasis is on mechanical aspects of the procedures rather than on teaching students why the procedures are necessary. Bennett (1992) comments that in 1985, "half of a course on Photo-fit construction was devoted to the psychology of memory and the eye-witness interview". Yet when questioned about teaching the insensitivity of photofit, a trainer said:

"That's a matter for the man who puts the picture together at headquarters. He should warn the officer in the case about the possibility of a poor likeness. We don't teach that."

Some might argue that at recruit/probationer level this kind of detail is unnecessary. The counter argument is that proper procedures which are difficult or time consuming to follow will be cut or avoided in damaging ways unless officers understand why they are as they are. Proper understanding is a powerful source of self-motivation to comply.

SUPERVISORY TRAINING

Suspects, Witnesses and Identification

In general terms, with the provisos noted above, coverage of the law and procedures dealing with suspects, witnesses and the conduct of identity parades and other forms of identification procedure, are adequately dealt with. However, the courses again do not tackle the question of why the procedures are necessary or identify in generic terms what they aim to achieve.

i) Sergeants:

Training sessions are devoted to "Introduction to supervision of investigations and interviews" (Session 4) and to "the custody officer" (Session 13). These sessions both use a role-play format and deal in the main with practical matters. The instructors' notes state an "objective" for Session 4 as:

> "This session is to allow the students the opportunity to explore the reasons why having sound "professional knowledge" is essential to be effective and efficient when supervising investigations" (Instructors Notes p.39)

The session aims to ensure "that students are aware of the necessity for close and diligent supervision of enquiries and investigations"; to "introduce the student to the concept of time management and organisation of work" and to identify what needs to be considered "when allocating tasks as a supervisor". In addition at the completion of the course (not the session) the sergeant should be able to demonstrate a number of elements of professional expertise. These are shown in Appendix 4.

Also included in the sergeants' course is a session (Session 22) on dealing with children and the mentally ill. This tends to concentrate on the content of the new Children Act 1989 and revolves around a case study dealing with an abused child. No mention appears to be made of the Community Care Act 1990 which will increasingly bring those defined as mentally handicapped into contact with the police for reasons other than criminal behaviour.

As a general rule, apart from material dealing with stress and stress management, the course does not deal with human factors issues and quality control in criminal investigation. The relationship between stress factors and error is not dealt with. There is no part of the course which presents supervision as a supporting and facilitating role. The necessity of such elements in supervision to maintain morale, reduce stress and control quality is not discussed.

ii) Inspectors:

As with sergeants' training, the inspectors' course is essentially pragmatic. There are practical inputs on running an identification parade and on the contents of PACE as they affect the Inspector (reviews, etc.). The whole course takes a thematic approach which is clearly demonstrated in the content of Appendix 5, which shows the "jigsaw-puzzle" construction of this style of training. The specific problem areas discussed in the introduction remain largely untouched.

SPECIALISED TRAINING (DETECTIVES/ INTERVIEWING SKILLS, ETC.)

Interview training

Background

Around 1984, following an initiative taken by the Merseyside Police, rapidly followed by a similar undertaking in West Midlands (Shepherd and Kite, 1988), police officers (mostly detectives) started to receive training in interviewing skills. However, two different models of police interviewing emerged. (Shepherd and Kite, 1988. pp.267–268): "the strategies" philosophy and "the managed communication" philosophy (Shepherd, 1986). There were also variations in the amount of training provided by different forces (Home Office Circular 22/1992).

The "strategies" philosophy rests on an assumption that the unwilling suspect needs to be manipulated towards confession by the use of "tactics" (Irving, 1980; Irving and McKenzie, 1989) or "strategies" (Hackett 1982; West Midlands Interview Development Unit, 1987; Walkley, 1987). The "managed communication" philosophy rests on the notion of "conversation management". Key concepts include: **rapport** (including attention and active listening); **regulation** (controlling the flow and content of a focused conversation), and **reasoning** (making sense of the entire interview), (Shepherd and Kite, 1988. pp.278).

A third approach has however gained pre-eminence in the psychological literature. The Cognitive Interview (CI), unlike the "strategies" and "managed communication" styles, has an extant and growing body of evaluation findings against which its claims can be assessed. The CI is defined by Memon and Bull (1991), as "a set of cognitive retrieval techniques designed to facilitate memory search (for example via reinstatement of contextual cues)".

George (1991), in a comparison between the cognitive interview, managed communication and the standard police interview, found that although managed communication will produce better results than the standard interview, the cognitive interview produced substantially more information than either of the other two methods.

The current position

Fisher, *et al.*, (1987) point out that the psychology of human memory is sufficiently advanced for it to be able to contribute to the investigation of crime in a practical way. The ACPO Working Party on Investigative Interviewing seized these reins and has set up a project team with the intention of seeking the best form of interviewing training for police officers in the UK.

Home Office Circular 22/1992 highlights some of the problem areas in this project and spells out the principles of "investigative interviewing". The document indicates that in June and July of 1992, four five-day pilot courses are to be run using materials and procedures currently defined as best practice. While some of the managed communication material will be included, it is likely that much of each course will concentrate on cognitive techniques, particularly in view of the comment in Circular 22/1992, that:

> "Investigative interviewing goes wider than the interviews of suspects addressed in the statutory guidance [PACE and the Codes of Practice]. It covers questioning at any stage in an investigation and includes questioning witnesses, suspects and victims. The fundamental principles of interviewing and basic interviewing techniques and skills are common to all these interviews. There is the same need for accurate, relevant and reliable information when questioning witnesses and victims as there is when questioning suspects..."

The Home Office is seeking to validate this training initiative.

DETECTIVE TRAINING GENERALLY

Background and history

The fragmented nature of current training in interviewing skills is echoed in detective training overall. Although there have been many initiatives in the last few years and whilst, like other training, the concentration is now on skills, on facilitated teaching and student centred learning, there is considerable potential for development. Unlike the recruit training facilities and those for sergeants and inspectors, the detective training programmes are run at detective training schools (Birmingham, Hendon, Preston, Wakefield, Merseyside, Bristol, Maidstone and Lewes) which are, in fact, force training schools which offer a service to other forces.

In a report by an ACPO sub-committee working to both ACPO Crime and Training Committees (ACPO, 1987) it was recommended that each detective training course should follow a standard syllabus at all training schools. Although the recommendations were accepted by ACPO and adopted by the various detective training centres, no monitoring mechanism was put in place. Consequently a "disparity" (Dickenson, 1992) has developed.

Bearing in mind the student-centred philosophy current in police training circles, this "disparity", consequent upon trainers' assessment of student-need, is inevitable. However, in recognition of that problem, a working group under the joint chairmanship of a member of ACPO Training Committee and ACPO Crime Committee, was set up (30 January 1991) to conduct a national review of CID training.

The working group is addressing all matters associated with detective training, but recognises that there is a need to provide training for *all* officers to ensure that they acquire basic investigation skills. This move is dictated by the high percentage of crime dealt with by uniform officers. On the recommendation of that group and with the involvement of the Central Planning Unit of the Home Office, research by the Metropolitan Police and the Kent Constabulary resulted in the design of a detective training course for provincial officers which has been piloted and validated. (A report is awaited). The course, based on that run by the Metropolitan Detective Training School for some years, has a pre-training school element in which, through examination on aspects of law and police procedure, and with a high cut-off score necessary for success, students are "filtered" onto the course. As with other training the course is skills based and student centred. It is anticipated that the course style, content and structure will be recommended as the model for all detective training schools.

Similar steps are in hand to re-structure training for supervisors of detectives (detective sergeants and detective inspectors) and it is recognised that there is a need to introduce systems to monitor, evaluate and re-assess all detective training to ensure appropriate standards are maintained and that the training offered continues to meet users' requirements.

Critique of detective training

In general the comments already made on recruit/probationer and uniform supervisory training are applicable to detective training. The overwhelming concentration is on mechanical aspects of law and procedure although these are comprehensively dealt with; the content of PACE and the Codes of Practice are covered with precision, case law is incorporated as soon as it is available, practical skills (including interviewing) are taught. However, students are not warned about human factors issues or instructed in the basics of quality control. There are inputs dealing with stress and stress management, but the associated problems beyond those of immediate supervision of a person so suffering, remain largely unaddressed. The link between stress and quality control is not covered. Similarly, relevant aspects of pure psychology including abnormal psychology, are conspicuous by their absence. As with other training, the issues discussed in the general introduction to this review remain largely untouched. Furthermore, according to an ACPO source, there are currently "in the teens of percent of young detectives who have received no specialist training".

TRAINING FOR SENIOR OFFICERS

As a direct consequence of the Byford Report (Home Office, 1982) on the investigation of the "Yorkshire Ripper" murders, recommendations were made with regard to the management of major crime investigations by senior police officers. These included:

a)   training of senior officers of ACPO rank,

b)   the recommendation that such officers should be freed of other responsibilities,

c)   the implementation and running of a senior management team, such management to be based on corporate management techniques,

d)   the appointment of a senior scientist as both a liaison with the Forensic Science Service and as an advisor to the officer in command,

e)   training in dealing with the media,

f)   the setting up of major incident rooms.

All these recommendations were accepted and are incorporated into training conducted at the Police Staff College in the SCIMITAR and Management of Serious and Series Crime courses. However, since the Byford Report other incidents have occurred and some have produced recommendations and consequent change.

The HOLMES (Home Office Large Major Enquiry System) system has become the standard tool for the management of major crime investigations. This computerised system replicates many of the procedures of the former "incident room" approach, and was developed with the following objectives (Dickenson & Stafford, 1991):

i)   to aid and improve the efficiency of the organisation of an incident room, and

ii)   to offer better information retrieval capabilities than those offered by the traditional card index

It is worth emphasising in this context that HOLMES is not an expert or intelligent system and depends for its effectiveness on the way it is run by human operators. As far as we know the error proneness of HOLMES operators and the way human errors affect the system have not been researched. Senior officers cannot therefore be armed with empirical evidence to help them in the management task.

Following a *post hoc* review of the Bamber Enquiry in Essex in 1986, additional recommendations (CHMI, 1986) designed to ensure proper management supervision and forming part of the SCIMITAR and Management of Serious and Series Crime courses were made, and include the following relevant item:

"Recommendation 16.

An officer of senior rank to the senior investigating officer will be available to attend briefings or meetings of staff in order to provide an objective assessment as to the progress of the investigation. This officer should avoid being fed the views of the senior investigating officer and take the opportunity at briefings, without undermining the command structure of the investigation, to question officers conducting specific areas of investigation."

Although SCIMITAR training encourages the practice of reviewing "undetected" murders (Whitehouse, 1992) it is unclear whether this is true of detected murders when it becomes clear at some point in the criminal justice process that quality control failures have occurred. It is also not clear whether such reviews are conducted in a manner likely to promote frankness about human factors issues. In addition, Whitehouse points out that such reviews are important, "in identifying faults in systems rather than identifying individuals who may not have performed properly". However, human factors reviews require the examination of the correlation between human and work system malfunctioning. The social psychological and technical components of the work system are not divisible. It appears to be taken for granted that individual errors are more the province either of the discipline system or of 'lady luck'.

Finally it remains uncertain whether a senior police officer is the appropriate person to conduct such *ad hoc* or *post hoc* reviews. While a senior officer should probably preside over proceedings, the technical tasks involved in such a review should be guided by experienced consultants independent of the service and having appropriate work study and human factors expertise.

CONCLUSIONS

At every level of police training there is considerable concern to modernise the approach and incorporate the most useful means of enhancing skill. Innovation in recruit and probationer training, in uniform and detective supervisor training, in specialised training for investigators and in senior officer training is abundant. As a senior officer at Chantmarle commented:

> "We think the training is better now than it's ever been. There are some flaws, of course, and some people don't like the system much. But I can't wait to see what the investigative interviewing package has to offer. We live in exciting times."

However, in the context of this report, it is important to question whether anything which could help reduce miscarriages of justice is being left out. It seems self-evident that knowledge about why a skill is essential is valuable in applying the skill: it will help the individual gauge what degrees of latitude are acceptable under extreme conditions. It will also help cope with the unexpected and bizarre. Knowing why also helps officers avoid the temptation to cut or avoid tedious procedures.

In addition there are important omissions of substantive information which might help officers at all levels deal with phenomena which are more properly the province of other professionals. Judgements have to be made about vulnerable suspects, so relevant instruction as to how to make such judgements needs to be provided otherwise the vacuum will be filled with dense PHOG (Prejudice, Hunch, Opinion and Guess).

There are now important bodies of knowledge in abnormal and forensic psychology which need translation into police training terms. This translation is an ongoing and specialised task. It has been suggested that such a speciality should be recognised and an appropriate resource located perhaps at the Police Staff College, Bramshill. So far this suggestion has been resisted. Without the development of a specialised body of useful knowledge police professionalisation is unlikely to progress.

Finally there are omissions which are perfectly understandable given current conceptualisations of police training needs but which may become significant if the arguments deployed in this study are accepted.

It is not current practice to teach or otherwise make students aware of their proneness to error. Although police officers operate under all kinds of difficult conditions, they are not taught how these conditions may affect the quality of either their own performance or that of the work systems of which they are a part.

In place of any finely tuned awareness of these issues, police officers are offered a clear understanding of their personal responsibility to perform to standard and a similar understanding of what the consequences will be if they do not. The formal sanctions available for failure are draconian. Informal sanctions can make working life extremely unpleasant. In contrast performing apparently up to standard can bring considerable rewards.

Such a system of whips and carrots can produce relatively successful results with little positive management effort. However, where operating conditions deteriorate, and if morale declines or the probability of errors being detected decreases, then this kind of strategy can quickly show its limitations.

It is time to assess whether or not some or all of these conditions now apply. If it is the view of the Royal Commission that they do, then supervisory training and aspects of general investigative training need re-thinking to incorporate the goal of proper awareness of human factors issues and the adoption of appropriate techniques of quality control. If and when these changes take place it should become apparent that the management of stress, now seen as a welfare function, is in reality an integral part of total quality management.

REFERENCES

ACPO (1987). ACPO CID Training Sub-Committee Review of Detective Training.

Bennett, P. (1992). Investigative Interviewing. Paper presented to the Investigative Psychology Seminar. Hendon Police Training College. 16th January 1992.

Bull, R., Bustin. R., Evans, P. and Gahagan, D (1983). *Psychology for Police Officers*. London: Wiley.

Bull, R. & Horncastle, P.(1983). *An evaluation of the Metropolitan Police training in Human Awareness Training.* London; Police Foundation.

Bruner, J.S. (1966). *Towards a theory of instruction.* Cambridge, Mass. Harvard university Press.

Burns-Howell, A.J., McKenzie, I.K. & Kember, R. (1981). Human Awareness Training for Recruits and Probationers. OG9/71/81. Metropolitan Police. October 1981.

CHMI (1986). Summary of recommendations made by HM Chief Inspector of Constabulary following the Bamber Case. London. Home Office.

Devlin LJ. (1971) *The Judge.*

Devlin Report (1976). *Report to the Secretary of State for the Home Department of the Departmental Committee of Evidence of Identification in Criminal Cases.* London; HMSO

Deffenbacher, K.A. (1980). Eyewitness accuracy and confidence. *Law and Human Behaviour.* 4, 243–260.

Dickenson, J.A. & Stafford, J.(1991). The management of serious and series crime investigations in England and Wales. Paper presented to a Homicide Seminar, FBI Academy, Quantico, VA. (17.12.91).

Dickenson J. (1992). Assistant HMIC. Personal communication.

Home Office (1982). HO Circular 114/82. The investigation of a series of major crimes.

Ellis, H.D. and Davis, G. with Shepherd, H. (1977). *An Investigation of the Photo Fit System for Recalling Faces.* Report to the Social Science Research Council.

Fisher, R.P. Geiselman, R.E., Raymond, D.S., Jurkevich, L.M., and Warhaftig, M.L. (1987). Enhancing eyewitness memory: refining the cognitive interview. *Journal of Police Science and Administration,* 15, 291–297.

Fontana, D. (1985). *Psychology for teachers.* Leicester; British Psychological Society.

George, R.C. (1991). A field and experimental evaluation of the three methods of interviewing witnesses/victims of crime. Unpublished Masters Dissertation.

Hackett, P. (1981 *Interview Skills and Training*. Institute of Personnel Management.

Home Office Circular, 22/1992. Principles of investigative interviewing.

Irving, B. (1980) *Police Interrogation: A case study of current practice*. London: HMSO.

Irving, B and McKenzie, I.K., (1989) *Police Interrogation: The Effects of the Police and Criminal Evidence Act 1984*

Loftus, E. and Palmer, J. (1974). Reconstruction of automobile destruction: An example of the interaction between language and memory. *Journal of Verbal Learning and Verbal Behavior*, 13, 585–589.

McDonald, B., Argent, M.j., Elliot, J.E., May, N.H., Miller, P.J., Naylor, J.T. and Norris N.F. (1986). Final Report of the Stage II Review of Police Probationer Training. University of East Anglia.

McKenzie, I.K. (1983). "Social Skills Training in a Police Context". Paper presented at BPS(London) Conference. Text published in DCLP Newsletter No.14 (April 1984).

McKenzie, I.K. (1984a). "Psychology and Police Training – A reply to Taylor", *Bull. Brit. Psychol. Soc.* 37, 145–147.

McKenzie. I.K. (1984b). "The requirements of his calling – Police training in the 1980s", *Police Journal*, Vol LVII, No 3.

McKenzie, I.K., Morgan R., and Reiner R. *Police Powers and Policy: A study of the work of custody officer.* (unpublished).

Memon, A. & Bull, R. (1991). The Cognitive Interview: Its origins, empirical support, evaluation and practical implications. *Journal of Community and Applied Social Psychology.* 1, 291–307/

Mirfield, P. (1985). *Confessions.* London; Sweet and Maxwell.

Moston, S., Stephenson, G.M. and Williamson T.M. (1990). Police interrogation: Styles and suspect behaviour. Report to the Police Requirements Support Unit.

Moston, S., Stephenson, G.M. and Williamson, T. (eds) (1991) *Investigative Interviewing.* In press

Shepherd, E. (1984). Values into practice: the implementation and implications of human awareness training. *Police Journal*, 57, 286–300.

Shepherd, E. (1986). The conversational core of policing. *Policing*. 2, 294–303.

Shepherd, E. and Kite, (1988). Training to interview. *Policing*, 4, 264–280.

Shepherd, J., Ellis, H.D. and Davis, G.M. (1982). *Identification Evidence: A Psychological Examination*. Aberdeen; Aberdeen University Press.

Walkley, J. Dressing up for the interview. *Police Review*. 93, 285–287.

West Midlands Interview Development Unit. (1987). *Students Course Manual*.

Whitehouse, P.C. (1992). Deputy Chief Constable West Yorks Police. Letter, *Independent* (6.2.92).

APPENDIX 1

Evaluation Criteria
Regional Training Centres

SKILLS

Desired Character Traits
1. Punctuality
2. Pride in appearance
3. Reliability
4. Concentration
5. Morally and physically courageous
6. Creativity
7. Self motivation
8. Attitudes towards others
9. Professional/personal responsibility

Monitoring Personal Performance
1. Self monitoring
2. Stress
3. Fitness/health
4. Learning from experience

Communication and Relationships with Others
1. Consideration of the feelings of others
2. Non-verbal communication (N.V.C. or body language)
3. Oral communication
4. Effective listening
5. Self control
6. Use of physical force
7. Relationships with others

Investigation
1. Assesses the total situation
2. Questioning
3. Collation and analysis of information

TASK

1. Using Radio
2. Answering Telephone
3. Document/Books
4. P.N.B. Entries
5. Statement Taking
6. Dealing with Property
7. Attending Scene of Crime No-one present
8. Someone present
9. Making an Arrest
10. Reporting an Offender
11. Executing Warrant
12. Serving Summons
13. Stopping Motor Vehicle
14. Administering First Aid
15. Talking to:– Offender
16. Victim
17. Witness
18. Delivering a Message
19. Preparation of File
20. Attending Scene of Accident
21. Preparing Sketch Plan
22. Preserving/Collecting Evidence
23. Public Order
24. Talking to Public
25. Searching:– People
26. Vehicles
27. Premises
28. Using Staff/Cuffs/Shields
29. Using Breath Test Device
30. Giving Evidence
31. Gaoler
32. Non-Offence Encounters

Knowledge

1. Knowledge of law
2. Knowledge of technical skills
3. Knowledge of procedures
4. Community awareness

Decision Making, Problem Solving, Planning

1. Decision making
2. Planning
3. Flexibility
4. Dealing with conflict and ambiguity

Practical Effectiveness

1. Initiative
2. Confidence
3. Responsibility
4. Leadership

Written Reports

1. Written reports

33. Seeking Advice
34. Checking Premises
35. Examination of Documents
36. Ejecting People
37. Sudden Deaths
38. Handling Dangerous Objects
39. Domestic Disputes

APPENDIX 2

DESIRED CHARACTER TRAITS

Punctuality
Pride in Appearance
Reliability
Concentration
Morally and Physically Courageous
Creativity
Self Motivation
Attitudes Towards Others
Professional/Personal Responsibility

MONITORING PERSONAL PERFORMANCE

Self Monitoring
Stress
Fitness/Health
Learning from Experience

COMMUNICATION AND RELATIONSHIPS WITH OTHERS

Consideration of the Feelings of Others
Non-Verbal Communication/NVC or Body Language
Oral Communication
Effective Listening
Self Control
Use of Physical Force
Relationships with Others

INVESTIGATION

Assesses the Total Situation
Questioning
Collation and Analysis of Information

KNOWLEDGE

Knowledge of Law
Knowledge of Technical Skills
Knowledge of Procedures
Community Awareness

DECISION MAKING/PROBLEM SOLVING/ PLANNING

Decision Making

Planning
Flexibility
Dealing with Conflict and Ambiguity

PRACTICAL EFFECTIVENESS

Initiative
Confidence
Responsibility
Leadership

WRITTEN REPORTS

Written Reports

APPENDIX 3

Climb the Thirty-Nine "Steps" to Independent Patrol

DOMESTIC DISPUTES
HANDLING DANGEROUS OBJECTS
SUDDEN DEATH
EJECTING PEOPLE
EXAMINATION OF DOCUMENTS
CHECKING PREMISES
SEEKING ADVICE
NON-OFFENCE ENCOUNTERS
GAOLER
GIVING EVIDENCE
USING BREATH TEST DEVICES
USING STAFF/CUFFS/SHIELDS
SEARCHING PREMISES
SEARCHING VEHICLES
SEARCHING PEOPLE
TALKING TO THE PUBLIC
PUBLIC ORDER
PRESERVING/COLLECTING EVIDENCE
PREPARING A SKETCH PLAN
ATTENDING A SCENE OF AN ACCIDENT
PREPARATION OF FILES
DELIVERING A MESSAGE
TALKING TO A WITNESS
TALKING TO A VICTIM
TALKING TO AN OFFENDER
ADMINISTERING FIRST AID
STOPPING A MOTOR VEHICLE
SERVING A SUMMONS
EXECUTING A WARRANT
REPORTING AN OFFENDER
MAKING AN ARREST
ATTENDING SCENES OF CRIME:– SOMEONE PRESENT
ATTENDING SCENES OF CRIME:– NO-ONE PRESENT
DEALING WITH PROPERTY
STATEMENT TAKING
P.N.B. ENTRIES
DOCUMENT/BOOKS
ANSWERING THE TELEPHONE
USING A RADIO

APPENDIX 4

At the end of this course, sergeants will be able to:–

1. Apply their knowledge and understanding of all relevant legislation, force directives and orders relevant to the investigation of offences, the questioning of suspects and the detention of prisoners.

2. Allocate responsibility for all matters requiring investigation and to supervise subsequent enquiries and submission of reports.

3. Direct officers in team situations to efficiently gather evidence and to co-ordinate the interviewing of suspects. To brief officers and to give instruction to achieve this aim.

4. Liaise with other supervisors, departments and agencies to ensure prisoners are promptly dealt with and enquiries and thoroughly and expeditiously concluded.

5. Ensure that the conduct of all officers engaged in the investigation/ supervision of any person in "police detention" is conducive to good discipline and in compliance with the Codes of Practice.

6. Properly to report to an officer of the rank of inspector or above of any complaint made by or on behalf of a detained person about his treatment since his arrest or improper treatment during detention.

7. When carrying out any or all of the above duties, responsibilities or tasks, demonstrate the supervisory skills required for effective:–

   • planning, organising and monitoring

   • problem solving and decision making

   • communication

   • leadership and motivation

   • job instructional techniques

   • performance management

   • time management

   • stress management

8. Transfer the knowledge and skills acquired during the course when dealing with supervision of investigations and interviews.

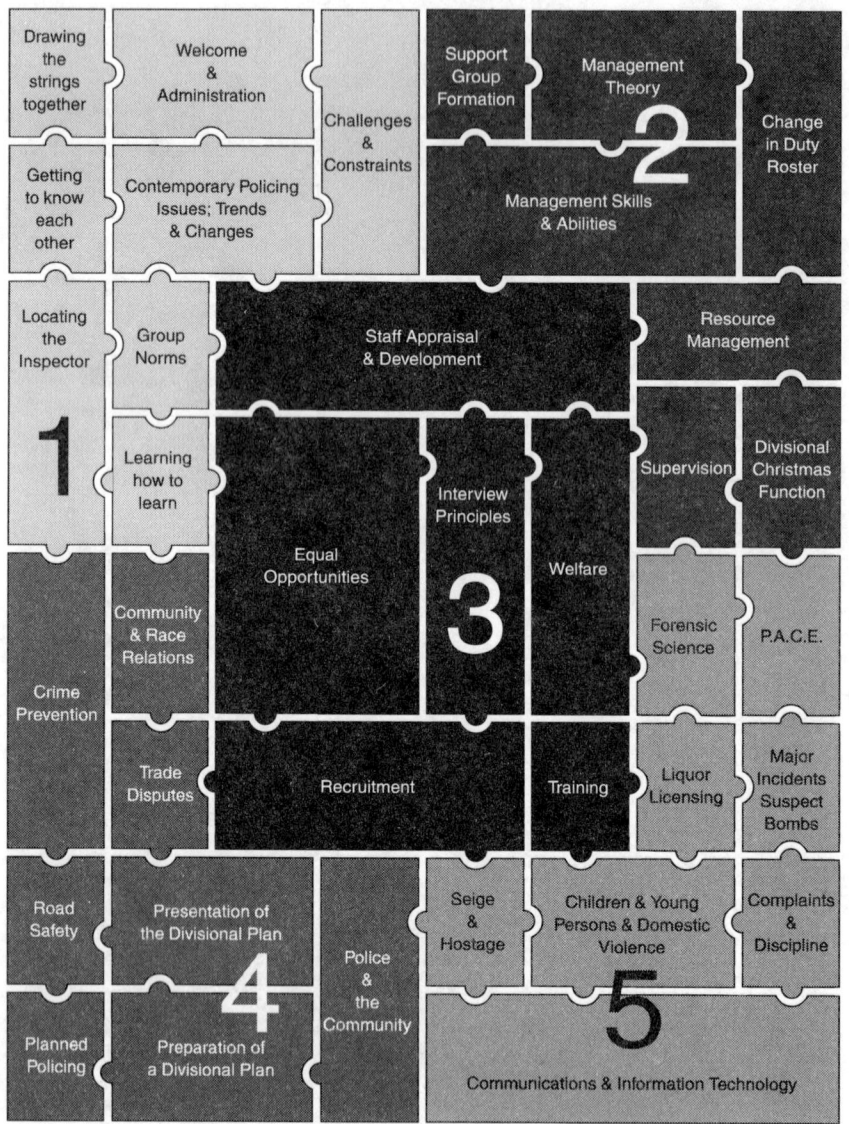

"A Guide to the 5 'Phases' of the Inspectors' Management Development Course"

Phase 1 = "CONTEXT AND ROLE"   Phase 2 = "MANAGEMENT SKILLS AND ABILITIES"
Phase 3 = "PEOPLE IN ORGANISATION"   Phase 4 = "POLICE IN THE COMMUNITY"
Phase 5 = "OPERATIONAL COMPETENCIES"

Printed in the United Kingdom for HMSO
Dd296491 8/93 C8 G3396 10170